Sounds Magnificent

Sounds Magnificent

The Story of the Symphony

HERBERT CHAPPELL

BRITISH BROADCASTING CORPORATION

Published by the
British Broadcasting Corporation
35 Marylebone High Street
London W1M 4AA

ISBN 0 563 20244 0

First published 1984
© Herbert Chappell 1984

Printed in England by
BAS Printers Limited
Over Wallop, Stockbridge, Hampshire
Colour originated by
Bridge Graphics, Hull,
and printed by Jolly & Barber Ltd,
Rugby

Contents

For Ben, Alison, Simon, Katy,
and Olivia

Foreword

The actual teaching of conducting is a fairly tenuous business. Conducting is, after all, the one musical endeavour that cannot be practised at home. Scores can be studied, parts marked, all the periphery prepared, but the actual guiding of an orchestra through repertoire can only be achieved with the players in front of you. With today's accessibility of good records and tapes, a great many young conductors make the cardinal error of waving their arms through a recorded performance, prior to facing living musicians playing the same piece, and invariably they are in for the shock of a lifetime. Unlike learning an instrument, being a conductor consists mainly of empirical knowledge.

During the summers, I teach at Tanglewood, the summer home of the Boston Symphony, and I do my best to recall my own student days, when I was extraordinarily lucky in having Pierre Monteux as my master. Monteux taught by indirection, by gentle (or not so gentle) hints, and by insisting that the conductor's goal should be the shaping of the phrase and not the beating of the meter. Some of Maître Monteux's pithy advice has stuck firmly in my head and comes back to caution me even now, after all these years. Let me give you only one example. In those fledgling years when I trudged off to my lessons with him, I was extremely proud of seeming very 'busy' on the podium. No entrance went uncued, no sforzando without a great theatrical gesture. However, one time I was given a Haydn symphony to conduct, with Monteux sitting quietly in the stalls. The last movement was a typical, rollicking presto in 2/4. As was my wont, I waved up a storm and leapt about. When it was over, Monteux beckoned to me. Very sweetly, he asked, 'Tell me, did you think the orchestra was playing well in the finale?' Fearing a trap, I stalled for a few seconds. Finally, and with trepidation, I said that yes, I thought they had played very well indeed. 'So did I,' offered Monteux; 'next time don't interfere!'

Well, a neophyte was never given better advice, and I've remembered it all my life. The incident flashed through my mind again last October, when the Royal Philharmonic and I met to rehearse a Haydn symphony for the upcoming series of television programmes called *Sounds Magnificent*. It was my first occasion of working with the RPO, whose invitation to become their Music Director I had happily accepted. A first rehearsal with a new orchestra is always a bit nerve-wracking for all the parties concerned. The conductor wants badly not to be eaten alive, and the orchestra is hoping that the new man on the rostrum will turn out to be all right. Happily, we got along famously, not only musically but personally, and now I am looking forward to a great number of concerts and records with that wonderful body of musical colleagues. Perhaps next time we can rehearse somewhere other than the hall across from Euston Station, where the lighting is that of a provincial seafood restaurant, with acoustics to match.

Obviously, any concert, whether in a world-famous hall or on television, rises or falls with the efforts and the expertise of the orchestral players. They deserve more credit than the conductor, and I want to thank the RPO for their generosity and their virtuosity, as well as their unfailing good nature under the hot lights. But in the case of this series for the BBC, I would be truly churlish if I weren't volubly grateful to Bert Chappell. Bert and I have worked together on various projects for almost seventeen years now and we know one another extremely well. He is a television director of enormous experience, he has a thorough knowledge of musicology, his set is always good-humoured and relaxed, the work goes quickly, and his crew would obviously be willing to make a film for him in Siberia during January. He is also a good composer and knows his way through a score page with an ease bordering on disdain. As you will see in this book, his scripts are admirable, easy to read and interesting to speak, and by now the two of us are almost able to finish each other's sentences like a practised music-hall team. I am very grateful to him and look forward to the next series with happy anticipation.

André Previn

Preface

It seems rather a long while ago that André Previn, contemplating one of his annually plotted and annually postponed sabbaticals, let slip that he hoped at least to take a few weeks away from conducting when he would have a rest and his wife Heather would have a baby.

Aided and abetted by Richard Somerset-Ward, Head of Music and Arts Programmes, and by Reiner Moritz, who co-produced the series, I felt this was a cue to script six ninety-minute programmes. The series would trace in broad strokes the development of the symphony and the growth of the orchestra. Ian Maclay, Manager of the Royal Philharmonic, crossed out existing commitments and wrote the single word 'television' across the RPO diary for the entire month of October 1983. The only question that remained concerned the estimated time of arrival of the new baby (who, André insisted, had prior booking). Would the newborn interrupt the recording of the Fifth Symphony of Dmitri Shostakovich or the Fantastic Symphony of Hector Berlioz? It had to be one or the other. Experienced punters in the percussion section anticipated a photo-finish and offered Berlioz as odds-on favourite, at thirteen to eight.

I had decided that each programme should include the performance of at least one complete symphony if the series was to have value. Having made that decision it was clear that we would inevitably leave out many important figures – Mahler, for example – and a number of minor composers, not least Carl Ditters von Dittersdorf, who wrote more symphonies than there are players in the Vienna Philharmonic.

As to the style of the scripts, there already existed far too many analytical accounts of symphonies, where music is explained in terms of formal structure. Such programme notes are more impenetrable than the leaflets sent with self-assembly kitchen cupboards – 'the inverted countersubject now reappears whimsically in the relative key of A Flat . . .' I felt that people of goodwill, innocently switching on their television sets, should be spared that sort of thing. Similarly, I assumed the audience had little need for musical terminology bewildering to anyone who is not a Radio 3 announcer or a waiter in an Italian restaurant.

Instead I approached the music from the viewpoint of the composer working in different historical periods. Looking at the environment, or in some cases the day-to-day circumstances, that shaped his career, I considered the composer's attitude towards other composers and towards his audience, the way he tackled his craft and handled the raw materials of melody, harmony, rhythm and orchestration. Such aspects of musical history always come across most vividly in letters, diaries and observations jotted down at the time by the composer's friends and colleagues. Consequently I have leaned heavily on sources – in some cases I have adapted them – and illustrations uncovered by scholars who have spent many years on dedicated research into their subject – Arthur Hutchings on Mozart, David Cairns and Peter Raby on Berlioz's relationship with Harriet Smithson, H. C. Robbins Landon on Haydn and Beethoven, and also Professor J. A. Westrup and Doctor Egon Wellesz, who guided for seven years my own research and postgraduate work at Oriel College, Oxford.

I am indebted to Sheila Lally, Marjorie Russell and Kathleen Darby, who worked on the television series, and to Tony Kingsford and his colleagues in BBC Publications for seeing this book into print. But most of all I thank my wife Julia for her constant help and encouragement, André Previn for his wise counsel and boundless good humour, and finally Heather Previn and baby Lukas. With impeccable timing, as befits a conductor's son, Lukas weighed in at seven pounds, ten and a half ounces, and precisely on cue – on the one free day in the entire recording schedule.

Herbert Chappell
March 1984

1

'An Ornament of Princes'

On 8 June 1781 the Archbishop of Salzburg finally lost patience with one of his employees and fired him. There is nothing very remarkable in that, except that the person he fired – a young musician in his mid-twenties – happened to be one of the supreme geniuses of all time. Taken by the scruff of the neck and physically booted into the street was Wolfgang Amadeus Mozart.

In the latter part of the eighteenth century composers still needed wealthy patrons; and in leaving the irksome duties of employment in the court of Salzburg Mozart was to face even greater frustration as a freelance musician in Vienna. There he lived out the last ten bitterly sad years of his life, dying at the age of thirty-five.

But for Joseph Haydn – the composer who more than anybody established the symphony and its related form the string quartet – the circumstances of patronage were different and congenial. For more than thirty years Haydn was a servant, but happily so. He was highly respected. He worked at Esterházy, near Vienna, resident composer to the richest family in Hungary. Born twenty-five years before Mozart, Haydn survived him by eighteen years. So both men lived through a period of European history when the role of the composer was changing fundamentally: from court-entertainer to creative artist – the difference between a servant in a grand household and an individual with a personal and committed voice.

In this book we shall examine that category of personal statement. It is tied up with the growth of the orchestra itself and it finds its most magnificent, its most elevated, expansive and powerful expression in that strange phenomenon we call 'the symphony'. But what do we mean by the symphony? And why has it achieved such a dominant place in the development of music over some 250 years? Beethoven's Fifth, Tchaikovsky's Pathétique and thousands of others are all 'symphonies', but otherwise have little in common.

The word itself has meant different things at different periods; at some points in its history the more precisely we try to define it, the greater the exceptions we need to quote. In the USA, for example, it describes not only a category of music but the orchestra itself. To

Date	City	Institution	Composition of Orchestra															Repertoire
			STRINGS					WOODWIND				BRASS			PERC.			
			Violins	Violas	Cellos	Double-basses	Viols	Flutes	Oboes	Clarinets	Bassoons	Horns	Trumpets/Cornet(t)s	Trombones/Tubas	Timpani/other	Keyboard	Plucked strings	
1607	Mantua	Gonzaga Palace, theatre	4	4	2	2	3	2				4/2	4		6	6		Monteverdi *Orfeo*
1634	London	King's Violins, masque	4	7	4													William Lawes
1670s–80s	Paris	24 Violons du Roi, Opéra	6	12	6			2	2		1		2		1	1		Lully operas
1728	London	King's Theatre	22	2	3	2		2	2		3	2				2	1	Handel operas
1730	Leipzig	Thomaskirche	6	4	2	1			3		2		3		1	2		Bach cantatas
1751	Paris	Opéra	16	6	7	5		2	3		4		1		1	1		Rameau
1754	Berlin	court	12	4	4	2	1	4	3		4	2	2		1	2	1	C. P. E. Bach. Quantz
1770s	Salzburg	court	18	2	2	1		1	2		3	2	2	3	1	1		Leopold and Wolfgang Mozart, Michael Haydn
1770s	Mannheim	court	20	4	4	4		3	3	3	4	4	2		1	1		Mannheim school, Stamitz, Mozart
1778	Paris	Concert Spirituel	22	6	9	6		2	2	2	2	2	2		1			J. C. Bach, Mozart, Haydn
1782	Vienna	court	12	4	3	3		2	2		2	2				2		Mozart, Salieri etc.
1783	Esterházy	court	10	2	2	2			2		2	2			1			Haydn
1791–3	London	Hanover Square Rooms	16	4	4	4		2	2		2	2	2		1	1		Haydn
1814	Vienna	Redoutensaal, concert	36	14	12	17		2	2	2	2	2	2	2	1			Beethoven
1814	Milan	Teatro alla Scala	25	6	4	8		2	2	2	2	4	2	1	1/1			Rossini
1824	Vienna	Kärntnertortheater, concert	24	10	6	6		2	2	2	2	2	2	2	1			Beethoven Ninth Symphony
1839	Leipzig	Gewandhaus, concert	17	5	5	4		2	2	2	2	2	2		1			Mendelssohn, Schumann
1839	Paris	Opéra	24	8	10	8		3	3	2	4	4	4	3	1/1			Meyerbeer, Halévy, Berlioz
1865	Leipzig	Gewandhaus, concert	30	8	9	5		2	2	2	2	4	2	3	1			Mendelssohn, Schumann etc
1876	Bayreuth	Festspielhaus	32	12	12	8		4	4	4	3	8	4	5	2/2		6	Wagner *Ring*
1876	Karlsruhe	court	18	4	4	4		2	2	2	3	4	2	3	1			Brahms First Symphony
1900	Vienna	Philharmonic Orchestra	33	11	10	10		4	4	4	4	8	4	5/1	2/3		1	Mahler, Strauss etc
1929	Dresden	State Opera	33	11	11	11		6	6	6	6	10	6	6/1	2/4			Strauss
1974	New York	New York Philharmonic, concert	34	12	12	9		4	4	5	4	6	4	4/1	2/3	2	1	Boulez, Carter

Note: This chart attempts to show the typical composition of orchestras for which works in the present-day repertoire were originally written. The figures have been drawn from standard reference works and from specialised studies. They must be taken as indicative in only a general sense, as forces varied from piece to piece, from occasion to occasion, and from year to year, as well as from place to place. To facilitate reference and comparison, instruments of the same families are grouped together without indication. Hence violins of all sizes appear in one column, as do: flutes, piccolos, alto flutes and recorders; oboes, English horns and tenor oboes; clarinets of all sizes; bassoons and double bassoons; trumpets and cornet(t)s; horns and Wagner tubas; and trombones of all sizes.

add to the confusion, a perfectly satisfactory symphony concert need not contain a symphony. Neither is there much in common between, say, Handel's Pastoral Symphony (from *Messiah*) and Beethoven's, or a symphony in a Monteverdi opera and another by Sibelius or Mahler. A symphony by Bruckner may last the best part of an hour and a half. Other composers – Anton Webern, for example – will condense the musical thought into just a few minutes.

And how do we account for the orchestra itself – eighty or a hundred musicians playing instruments made from materials that have changed very little over the centuries: wood, metal, horsehair and gut? The modern symphony orchestra – eight dozen musicians dressed as penguins, scraping, banging or blowing an identical selection of instruments, seated in much the same way on concert platforms in every major city in the world – is a relatively recent invention. Such an orchestra was unknown to Bach and Handel. Today – 250 years later – it often appears to be dying out, an expensive anachronism in an age of synthesisers, computers and electronic wizardry. So why does the symphony orchestra retain such a dominant position in musical life?

As an institution its present position is vulnerable. In many major musical centres audiences have been falling off. No orchestra can exist purely on revenue from ticket sales; it needs other sources of income – from recording, film or television contracts, commercial sponsorship, friendly millionaires or government subsidy, or all of them. The musicians are paid to produce the most intangible end-product imaginable – sounds that disappear into thin air. But these days, unlike earlier generations, orchestral players expect to receive a weekly wage, statutory holidays, retirement pensions and regular employment like other members of the community. As a way of life, an orchestral player must be prepared to go to work at the time of day when any sane person is returning to the bosom of his family. It can also be assumed that he has devoted the earlier part of his day to rehearsal, instrumental practice, teaching or 'session' work, often playing mediocre music that he will have sight-read impeccably. Aesthetically, symphony orchestras today are difficult institutions to justify for they stay in business only by playing old-fashioned music written by people who died a long time ago. Lacking the cash to be more daring, they churn out a fossilised repertoire of museum pieces, culled from a few dozen compositions which are already available in a wide selection of recordings by other orchestras. Technologically,

The fourteen-year-old
Louis XIV as the Sun King in
Le Ballet de la Nuit.

the appearance of the instruments themselves seems more suited to a science museum – tubes, pistons, levers, pieces of wood glued together – all somewhat quaint in an age of microprocessors, interactive cable systems and trips around the galaxy. There are a thousand valid question marks, yet the sound of a symphony orchestra retains that same primeval, thrilling potency that goes back deep in our history. In Biblical times a brass band of 120 musicians, we are told, celebrated the dedication of Solomon's Temple, and all these trumpeters constituted only a part of the ensemble; dozens of other musicians were there too, playing cymbals, harps and zithers, while an enormous choir sang songs of praise.

Nearer to our own time, every prince of the Renaissance flattered his guest, and his own ego, with the impact of music. Indeed, the whole point of opera – as it originated and developed – was to entertain and impress, by its lavishness and its spectacular effects. One of the prototypes of the modern orchestra is to be found in the magnificent courtly pomp of Versailles, in the reign of Louis XIV, the Sun King. Earlier in the seventeenth century, Monteverdi and other Italian composers who pioneered the expansion of opera had used exotic and dramatic instrumental colours that favoured plucked instruments, woodwind, brass and keyboards, as well as a large number of stringed instruments played with bows. But at the court of Louis XIV the opulence and the variety of music-making was to reach staggering proportions in the hands of a charming and capable young Florentine. He arrived at the French court in the spring of 1646, aged thirteen. Soon he impressed one and all with his growing range of talents: dancer, guitarist, composer, actor, harpsichordist and violinist of the first rank. Jean-Baptiste Lully (often shortened to 'Baptiste') was a superstar:

> Mais pour danse et pour mélodie,
> Il faut, toutefois, que je dis,
> Que Baptiste, en toute façon,
> Est un admirable garçon.

When Lully was twenty, he and Louis XIV – a fourteen-year-old stripling – appeared together, dancing in the same ballet. Lully quickly established himself as France's leading composer, in charge of all the king's musical entertainments, operas, ceremonial music and church services. It was a position of immense importance. There was no shortage of musicians on the payroll, which included woodwind

Lully became one of the most
influential musical figures of
the time.

and brass players from the military bands and from the royal stables. But above all, the pride of the court was a group of twenty-four string-players whose fame had spread over Europe – the Vingt-quatre Violons du Roi, organised in 1626 by Louis XIII.

Lully's musicianship had full rein. His achievements with such a large orchestra were envied in all the courts of Europe, especially in London. In 1660 Charles II ascended the English throne after exile in the French court, and set out to organise his own music-making on similar lines. In London at that time, concerts open to the public had become a fashionable way of spending the afternoon. London society under Charles II can take much credit for this idea of *public* concerts, which was something quite new. In organising his own string orchestra to rival that of Louis XIV at Versailles, Charles II was to place an official seal of approval, as it were, on the very status of music as a profession. The *London Gazette* of 30 December 1672 carried an advertisement from John Banister, one of King Charles II's 'Band of 24 Violins':

Above: A member of Louis XIV's band of string players, the Vingt-quatre Violons du Roi, who provided music for all types of occasion at Versailles.

These are to give notice that at Mr John Banister's house (now called the music school) over against the George Tavern, in White Friars, near the back of the Temple, this Monday, will be performed music by excellent masters, beginning precisely at 4 of the clock in the afternoon, and every afternoon in the future, precisely at the same hour.

Left: A performance before the king, queen and dauphin of Lully's opera *Alceste* in the marble courtyard of Versailles. The opera was premièred in 1674.

Banister charged his audience a shilling, which included as much ale and tobacco as they could consume. Understandably, concerts such as these became all the rage. Impromptu concerts given in alehouses by itinerant musicians had a long and disreputable history, but Banister's musicians — and the sort of music they performed — were a cut above such hobbledehoys. To make it clear to all that these were no mere wandering buskers, Banister placed his band on a raised dais and behind a curtain.

The term 'violin' — in London as much as at Versailles — in Banister's time covered stringed instruments of differing sizes. The players were grouped into six violins and six cellos; the remaining dozen players were divided into three groups of different-sized violas — small, medium and large. Thus, at Versailles and in London, the idea of a string orchestra, playing as a unified ensemble, became an accepted and respected feature of musical life from around 1630 onwards. Its purpose was to accompany dramatic performances, masques, ballets, odes and anthems, supplemented by trumpets and kettledrums when the music demanded a celebratory panache.

In France in the latter half of the seventeenth century, largely due to Lully's influence, the quality of woodwind playing also improved out of all recognition, thanks to mechanical refinements introduced by two Parisian families. Hotteterre and Chédeville were wind instrument makers and repairers who redesigned the older type of Renaissance flutes, recorders, oboes and bassoons. These new models were easier to play in tune and they produced a more even tone throughout their range of notes. In addition to the Vingt-quatre Violons du Roi, Versailles also boasted the Douze Grands Hautbois, employed in the royal stables for processional and ceremonial occasions, out in the open air, where the fragile tone of stringed instruments would blow away in the breeze. These *hautbois*, a wind group of ten oboes and two bassoons, could reinforce the melody and the bass-line of the string orchestra. The end of the seventeenth century saw horns and double-basses assume their position in the orchestra.

Although all the essential instruments of the orchestra were thus readily available by the start of the eighteenth century, there was no need for conformity between one orchestra and the next, since they shared no common repertoire of music. On the contrary, the printing and distribution of full orchestral scores and instrumental parts was unheard of. In the absence of any laws regarding copyright protection, composers jealously guarded their manuscripts. Journeys between countries were hazardous and expensive since currency lost value every time a traveller crossed the border into the next principality. Consequently, most music composed up to the start of the eighteenth century was written for specific performances, tailored to the capability and the availability of particular groups of musicians working in particular places at particular times. There was no idea of writing for posterity, or for a standardised orchestra. Before the French Revolution, Europe was a motley, feudal patchwork of dukedoms, principalities and kingdoms, each with its own entourage of courtiers, petty officials, hangers-on and, yes, musicians. In such circumstances, the growth of a symphonic repertoire only became possible when working conditions were stable enough for an orchestra of skilled players to flourish in the same place over several generations. Those conditions would soon become possible through a freak of history.

Mannheim stands on the banks of the Rhine in what is now West Germany. In the eighteenth century it housed the court of the Elector Palatine and was regarded as a showplace. Freshly designed with parallel streets (a novel concept at the time) it was a town planner's dream. It became an essential stopping-off point for travellers from all over Europe brave enough to tackle the Rhineland section of the Grand Tour.

Particularly famous was the Mannheim orchestra, renowned for its immaculate precision, something unheard-of in the middle of the eighteenth century. Many of the players were equally skilled composers whose symphonies developed many exciting effects, each with

The orchestration of Vivaldi is picturesque and captivating, but for two hundred years after his death he was virtually unknown to the general public. Today recordings of his works fill twelve closely typed columns in gramophone catalogues.

The palace at Mannheim.

its own particular nickname. There was the 'Mannheim steamroller' – a progressive crescendo. There were bustling arpeggios, known as the 'Mannheim skyrockets', that shot up through the orchestra. And when Mozart spent four and a half months at Mannheim in 1777, he was bowled over by the variety and skill of the woodwind playing, and by the 'Mannheim sigh' – an expressive melodic turn of phrase. The orchestra was the pride and joy of Karl Theodor, Elector Palatine, a benevolent patron of art, science and commerce.

The palace itself was grandly designed, far superior to the ruins of Heidelberg with its bickering burghers and cramped, pock-marked castle, irreparably damaged during the War of the Spanish Succession. Inevitably, like any new centre of government, Mannheim quickly developed its own bureaucracy as soon as the court of the Elector moved there from Heidelberg just before Christmas 1720. At the outset economy was the watchword. But the expensive tastes of the Elector Karl Philipp – and, after 1742, his successor Karl Theodor – were soon asserted. Within a few years of the move from Heidelberg nearly sixty musicians were on the payroll. During thirty-five years of untroubled peace Mannheim attracted three generations of the best talents in Europe: Italian opera designers like the Galli-Bibiena family, and musicians like Johann Stamitz from Czechoslovakia and his brilliant sons, virtuoso composers and violinists. Mannheim quickly became a tourist centre:

Numbers of well-dressed people were amusing themselves with music and fireworks in the squares and open places. Other groups appeared conversing in circles before their doors, and enjoying the serenity of the evening. Almost every window bloomed with carnations; and we could hardly cross the street without hearing a German flute.

William Beckford's enthusiasm is reflected in the comments of other travellers, most of whom were unrestrained in their praise of the Elector's generosity, his sense of style and the lavishness of his hospitality. The summer palace alone, at the tiny village of Schwetzingen just a few miles from Mannheim, supported an entourage of 1500 people in considerable style.

However, James Boswell, Dr Johnson's biographer, was less impressed. According to him, the Elector's wife was 'much painted' and the Elector himself was 'very high and mighty'. 'What an inhospitable dog!' he wrote. 'I have been obliged to dine amongst fellows of all sorts and sizes. The company disgusted me sadly.' Boswell was rather annoyed not to have received an invitation to dine with the Elector.

Karl Theodor, Elector
Palatine.

His account of Mannheim concludes scathingly: 'O British, take warning from me and shun the dominions of the Elector Palatine.'

The Elector Karl Theodor, according to other accounts, was a paragon. The critic Daniel Schubert wrote:

It would be hard to find another great man who has woven music into his life as this one. Music wakes him, music accompanies him to table, music resounds when he goes hunting, music wings his worship in church; music lulls him in balmy slumber, and it is hoped that at the end it greets this truly good prince at the gates of heaven.

Karl Theodor, a skilled player on several instruments, eventually employed as many as ninety musicians, a considerable number by any standard. Operatic productions were lavish; the Mannheim orchestra was disciplined and imaginative: an orchestra, it was said, 'with more solo players and composers than any other in Europe. An army of generals — equally fit to plan a battle as to fight it.' But

Mannheim was unique. With that combination of enthusiasm, talent and money (what better ingredients for the arts to flourish?) it was the envy of more modest establishments, and a rival to Versailles itself. When Voltaire's secretary first visited the town in 1753, it was claimed that the Palatine Court was then probably the most brilliant in Germany. One festivity followed the next: 'There were hunts, operas, French plays and musical performances by the first virtuosos of Europe.'

A magnificent opera-house seating 5000 was built in the palace. The scenic effects were spectacular; the singers were the finest money could buy – though Mozart for one felt some of them were past their best. The gardens of the summer palace at Schwetzingen rivalled Versailles. Charles Burney, the English musical historian, writing at the time, conjures up a scene as idyllic as a gentle summer evening at Glyndebourne:

The going out from the opera at Schwetzingen during the summer into the electoral gardens – which, in the French style, are extremely beautiful – affords one of the gayest and most splendid sights imaginable. The country here is flat and naked and therefor would be less favourable to the free and open manner of laying out grounds in English horticulture, than to that which has been adopted. The orangery is larger than that at Versailles, and perhaps than any other in Europe.

It was in such circumstances that the arts flourished. Almost as a by-product the pre-Classical symphony was spawned from the opera overture and the orchestral suite. But while Mannheim flourished, the love of opera reached disastrous proportions in the neighbouring principality of Württemberg. The Duke of Württemberg was an opera buff of the most extravagant kind. As a result, his entire state went bankrupt. In Mannheim, too, the funds to run an opera-house, and an orchestra of such distinction, had to come from somewhere. The expense of wax candles to light just one performance alone was enough to ruin an average monarch. Charles Burney pointed out that 'the palaces and offices extend over almost the town; and one half of the inhabitants, who are in office, prey on the other, who seem to be in the utmost indigence'.

Johann Stamitz, who was responsible for the orchestra, was famed as a brilliant violinist long before he joined the Elector's court. Throughout his long career, Stamitz had but one brief to follow: to attract to Mannheim the best musicians possible. With his sons Philipp and Anton he built up a magnificent tradition of musicianship and technique. In August 1772 Dr Burney had found the Mannheim orchestra 'to be indeed all that its fame had made me expect; power will naturally arise from a great number of hands; but the judicious use of this power, on all occasions, must be the consequence of good discipline'. Clearly, Stamitz possessed both a fine technique and the qualities of an outstanding orchestral trainer, able to produce in his string section a unique precision of attack and subtlety of phrasing. The German poet Schubart, a journalist and composer banished by the Duke of Württemberg for his dissolute behaviour when employed as harpsichordist in the ill-fated Württemberg opera-house, quite idolised the achievements of Stamitz:

He has invented a totally new bowing technique and possesses the gift of holding the largest orchestra together by nothing more than the nod of his head and the movement of his elbows. He is really the creator of the smooth tone characteristic of the Palatine orchestra. He is the inventor of all the magical devices that are now admired by the whole of Europe. No orchestra in the world has ever excelled the Mannheim. Its forte is a thunderclap, its crescendo a cataract, its diminuendo a crystal stream babbling away in the distance, its piano a breath of spring. The wind instruments are everything they should be; they raise and carry or fill and inspire the storm of the strings.

The origins of modern attitudes to ensemble, phrasing, balance and attack in orchestral playing can be found in this magnificent period at Mannheim. The 'magic island of sound', as Schubart described it, owed much to the way Stamitz and his fellow composers used the woodwind instruments of the orchestra. French and Italian opera had long displayed the expressive tone-colours of woodwind instruments, but the Mannheim composers took matters further in two important respects.

The first difference lay quite simply in the actual number of wind players – considerably greater than was customary. Consequently, the internal balance of the tone-colours and the distinction between stringed instruments and the woodwind sounded refreshingly new. Secondly and more importantly, the Mannheim composers exploited the individual characteristics of the different woodwind instruments, their tonal qualities and the expressiveness of solo passages. This had not been possible earlier, for it was not until the latter half of the eighteenth century that the design of woodwind instruments generally improved. Craftsmen and instrumentalists were beginning to produce instruments with refinements that made them technically superior to earlier models, more reliable and easier to play in tune.

In Bohemia, the *cors de chasse* – an indispensable part of any

For generations of composers – up to and including Brahms – the design of the orchestral horn was little different from the eighteenth-century hunting horn shown here.

Hapsburg hunting lodge – produced horn players of great skill. In France, oboe players were good and plentiful. In Berlin, at the court of Frederick the Great, flute playing was in a class of its own – not least because Frederick himself was a flautist of relentless enthusiasm and considerable technical skill. A letter home from Mozart confirms that Mannheim contained woodwind players of a very high standard. He was most impressed by the sound of the clarinet, which was for him a completely new experience: 'Oh, if only we also had clarinets in Salzburg. You cannot imagine the beautiful effect of a symphony with flutes, oboes and clarinets.' This was the start of Mozart's lifelong delight in the warm, golden sound of the clarinet, an instrument he understood to perfection. Indeed, so enthusiastic was he about the skill of the woodwind players at Mannheim that he composed for them some of his most endearing and enduring music, where his deepest thoughts find expression not merely in the written notes, but in the very tone-colour of the instruments themselves.

But Mozart's admiration for the woodwind players of Mannheim contrasts oddly with the remark of Dr Burney who noted 'the want of truth [i.e. intonation] in the wind instruments'. The good doctor confessed it was natural in those days for woodwind instruments to play out of tune on occasions, but perhaps he himself was out of sorts or encountered the players on a bad night.

Mozart himself never tired of the exciting musical atmosphere of Mannheim, which he visited on four separate occasions and where he hoped for employment. Aged twenty-one, he was there on New Year's Eve 1777 when the Palatine court moved to Munich. (Maximilian II had died and Karl Theodor had inherited the Electorate of Bavaria.) The Mannheim orchestra was disbanded, the opera-house closed and the musicians paid off. Many later found work in Vienna, where another generation of symphonists flourished. With his mother, Mozart watched the courtly exodus and in a letter to his father in Salzburg, he wrote: 'Here, now, it is dreadfully quiet and ever so boring . . .'

2
'A Little Monsieur with a Wig and a Sword'

Until quite late in the eighteenth century public concerts were a novelty. A composer, therefore, stood little chance of getting his music performed unless he was part of a royal or aristocratic household. This was a fact of musical life. No matter how great the composer, without a patron he was nobody.

This was why Mozart's father toured with his two children around Europe like a circus act, endlessly hob-nobbing with potential patrons who might offer the young Mozart a job one day – preferably as Kapellmeister, where he would have his own orchestra and possibly even his own opera-house. It was a harsh childhood but it helps us understand how Mozart developed such a phenomenal technique as a composer, virtually from the cradle.

Mozart's father, Leopold, was a highly respected musician in the court at Salzburg. He was also an expert on violin playing, famous as the author of a treatise on the subject. Both children – Wolfgang, and his sister Nannerl, four and a half years his senior – were infant prodigies, educated entirely by their father. Leopold, who has often been maligned, was an excellent teacher. He was determined that Wolfgang should be successful, and to that end he largely sacrificed his own career. When Nannerl was very young, Leopold compiled a book of little keyboard pieces for her. Obviously Wolfgang also used the book because the proud father scribbled in the margin comments such as: 'Wolfgang learnt this minuet on 26th January, in half an hour, at half past nine in the evening, one day before his fifth birthday.'

At the age of four Wolfgang was playing the piano and teaching himself the violin; at six he was composing little minuets; at nine he was writing symphonies and at twelve his first opera. But he did not learn to do this at a tiny desk, quill pen in hand, a Dresden doll in a sound-proofed room, cocooned from the outside world. On the contrary, Mozart's formative years were spent travelling around Europe in stage-coaches on dangerous, potholed roads with one-night stops at wayside inns. The children were often exhausted and frequently ill. In each place they waited around, hoping to impress

Wolfgang Amadeus Mozart. (Posthumous portrait by Barbara Krafft)

Travel in eighteenth-century Europe was dangerous and expensive. There was constant risk of attack from highwaymen and currency lost value at every border.

some dignitary or other with their party pieces. Leopold would get the children to play duets with a cloth covering their hands, so that neither child might see the keys – not, as it happens, all that difficult a trick, but astonishing enough in a six-year-old and quite good enough to impress the grand families they encountered – potential patrons on whom Wolfgang would soon have to depend. Two weeks before Wolfgang's sixth birthday, the Mozart family left home in Salzburg on the first of several promotional tours. They headed for Munich and travelled along the Danube – through violent storms with the river in flood – to Vienna, where Wolfgang celebrated his seventh birthday in bed with rheumatism.

Soon they were on their travels again – this time for three and a half years. Leopold bought a portable keyboard instrument so that the children might keep up their practice in wayside inns and overnight stops. They went to Mannheim, Mainz and Frankfurt, where the seven-year-old Mozart impressed the fourteen-year-old Goethe – who later remembered him as a 'little monsieur with a wig and a sword'. Then it was back to Mainz, Koblenz, Bonn, Cologne, Aix-la-Chapelle to Brussels – where Leopold and his family, their cash running low, waited for a month to be received by the Emperor's brother, Charles of Lorraine. 'This fine prince,' said Leopold bitterly, 'does nothing but hunt, eat like a pig, and drink.'

The Mozarts all this time were living in awful circumstances. 'There was a pot on a long chain,' said Leopold, 'with meat, turnips and all manner of things boiling together. The door was left open, so we were honoured by visits from the pigs, who grunted all around us.' Eventually, they were graciously received and, on this occasion, rewarded handsomely. But it was not always like this. Often as not the children's party piece attracted delighted ripples of applause, a pat on the head, and yet another bauble. 'What with snuff boxes and leather cases and such trumpery, we shall soon open a shop. But neither the innkeeper nor the postmaster can be paid by kisses,' wrote Leopold.

They left Brussels for Paris, where they stayed for five months, showered with invitations as the nobility vied to entertain Wolfgang. On Christmas Eve they arrived at Versailles and were invited to stay a fortnight and to attend a magnificent banquet with the royal family on New Year's Day. Leopold made a lot of money from the Versailles trip, but the rewards were not exclusively financial. It was there that Wolfgang encountered some of the finest musicians of the age – com-

A view of Salzburg.

posers and instrumentalists from Germany and Italy — who were employed at the court.

Soon after Wolfgang's eighth birthday they headed for England, leaving France via Calais. The family stayed in London, where Wolfgang met the undisputed king of London's musical world, Johann Christian, youngest son of J. S. Bach. Although born in Germany, J. C. Bach wrote music in the Italian style, which was all the rage. He was also an impresario — one of the first to promote public orchestral concerts. While he was in London, Wolfgang's compositions absorbed in a remarkable way the mature characteristics you would not ordinarily associate with a child of eight or nine. No doubt his father was influential in this, but the boy's talent was nevertheless phenomenal. He and his sister had a splendid time and Nannerl's diaries, charmingly misspelt, talk about their sightseeing at 'St Paul Kirch', 'Linconsin fiels' and 'Soumerset haus'.

After fifteen months in London, the family left for Holland, travelling via Canterbury and Dover to The Hague, where Nannerl, now fourteen, was so ill with typhus she was given the last rites. Wolfgang also contracted typhus and, although they both survived, he was ill from November through to the spring, often delirious and in a coma. Eventually they headed for home, via Amsterdam, Utrecht, Antwerp, Brussels, Paris and Versailles again, down to Dijon and Lyons into

Johann Christian Bach, J. S. Bach's youngest son, who settled in London, where he dominated the musical life after Handel's death in 1759. (Gainsborough)

Switzerland — Geneva, Lausanne and Berne to Zurich — and then to Munich. Not surprisingly, Wolfgang was again ill.

Today we complain of delays at airports and traffic jams on motorways, but twentieth-century travellers cannot appreciate the hazards of travel in the eighteenth century: the need to change horses every few hours; jolting over muddy roads; the cold, the danger, the exhaustion of moving from one inn to the next; making detours to avoid villages where there was an outbreak of smallpox or typhus. But for Mozart more journeys were to come — to Italy, Vienna and other places. It is not difficult to imagine the impression these journeys made on such a sensitive and receptive little boy. Before the age of fifteen his experiences included Christmas at Versailles; a private audience with the Pope; Venice in the carnival season; the art and architecture of Florence, Bologna, Verona, Rome; Pompeii and Vesuvius. Leopold, it must be remembered, was a man of culture who loved books, paintings and sightseeing. It is doubtful — certainly in

To all Lovers of Sciences.

THE greateſt Prodigy that Europe, or that even Human Nature has to boaſt of, is, without Contradiction, the little German Boy WOLFGANG MOZART; a Boy, Eight Years old, who has, and indeed very juſtly, raiſed the Admiration not only of the greateſt Men, but alſo of the greateſt Muſicians in Europe. It is hard to ſay, whether his Execution upon the Harpſichord and his playing and ſinging at Sight, or his own Caprice, Fancy, and Compoſitions for all Inſtruments, are moſt aſtoniſhing. The Father of this Miracle, being obliged by Deſire of ſeveral Ladies and Gentlemen to poſtpone, for a very ſhort Time, his Departure from England, will give an Opportunity to hear this little Compoſer and his Siſter, whoſe muſical Knowledge wants not Apology. Performs every Day in the Week, from Twelve to Three o'Clock in the Great Room, at the Swan and Hoop, Cornhill. Admittance 2s. 6d. each Perſon.

The two Children will play alſo together with four Hands upon the ſame Harpſichord, and put upon it a Handkerchief, without ſeeing the Keys.

An English newspaper advertising a concert at the Swan and Hoop, Cornhill, where Mozart and his sister played duets.

the eighteenth century – if any other child had the chance to encounter so much of the musical world around him, to meet so many composers and instrumentalists, to soak up so many different musical styles and attitudes from one country to the next. Throughout all this, Wolfgang had learned to write reams and reams of music – apparently with great speed and effortless facility – whatever the circumstances, as part of his daily routine.

At fifteen Mozart was a self-confident teenager, but his days as a child prodigy were numbered. Leopold was already beginning to knock a year off the boy's age. Wolfgang too was beginning to see himself in a new light. Had he not proved to the world and to himself that everything his father said was true – that he was indeed a miracle child, a gift from God? Had he not been received by kings and emperors, princes and ambassadors?

Leopold instilled in his children the need not only to do well, but to be seen to be doing well, to let everybody know they were artists, not mere court buskers. So, throughout his life Wolfgang was very careful about his appearance, dressing neatly and well, wearing clothes that almost certainly cost more than he could really afford and which showed he was used to moving in aristocratic circles. He was about five foot four in height, with blue eyes and light brown, fair hair. Smallpox had damaged his complexion, but it did not prevent him enjoying dancing and good company. Kidney trouble gave his skin a yellowish tinge, particularly when his health deteriorated in his last years. He had a great sense of humour, loved smutty jokes and was blessed with a colourfully obscene vocabulary, infantile and lavatorial. He liked to work late into the night and possessed extraordinary stamina, until uraemia started to sap his strength.

In his lively *Reminiscences* Michael Kelly, the Irish opera singer who appeared in Vienna in Italian opera under the name Signor Occhelli, tells us that Mozart was

a remarkable small man, very thin, with a profusion of fine fair hair, of which he was rather vain. He gave me a cordial invitation to his house, of which I availed myself and passed a great deal of my time there. He always received me with kindness and hospitality. He was remarkably fond of punch, of which beverage I have seen him take copious draughts. He was also fond of billiards and had an excellent table in his house. Many and many a game have I played with him, but always came off second best.

(From A. Hutchings, *Mozart, The Man, The Musician*, Thames and Hudson, 1976)

We also know that he was good at mathematics and the education he received from his conscientious father was far better than if he had attended a choir school like Haydn and Schubert did. Wolfgang was a good Latin scholar and could read and converse in Italian, French and German.

Because of the great speed with which Mozart composed music, it has often been assumed, quite incorrectly, that it came to him easily, and flowed on to the paper without any trouble. On the contrary, he probably found the composition process no easier than did Beethoven, whose struggle with the raw materials is well documented in manuscript sketchbooks. But Mozart's method was to work out every detail in his head and then – with the structure, harmonic progressions and melodic ideas settled – to commit the whole thing to paper, rarely changing anything. This might have been a natural gift, but such fluency also came from technique acquired through habit; it should not be confused with mere facility. He was often known to excuse himself from the dinner table, reappearing at the end of the meal having written out an entire section of music, complete and fully orchestrated. Wolfgang, even when engaged on routine activities, 'was swallowed up in music, busy with it all day long, speculating, studying, considering'.

From the very start he was extremely sensitive to sound. It is said that as a child he could tell when a violin was tuned incorrectly by as little as one eighth of a tone – an extremely fine distinction, virtually inaudible, even to a fully trained musician. Until he was ten the sound of a trumpet filled him with terror. Andreas Schachter, the Salzburg court trumpeter and one of Leopold's fellow musicians, recounted:

If one merely held a trumpet towards him, it was like pointing a pistol at his heart. His Papa wanted to cure this childish fear and asked me to sound the trumpet towards him. My God! I wish I had never let myself be persuaded! As soon as Wolfgang heard the piercing tone he turned pale and started to faint.

(From A. Hutchings, *Mozart*)

This act, which smacks of cruelty, tells us more about Leopold than about Wolfgang. Leopold saw himself as neither an autocrat nor a bully but as a man who simply wanted the best for his son. Within the structure of eighteenth-century society, a composer depended entirely upon the whim of his patron. Musicians were not recompensed with royalties and fees for copyright, performances and the distribution of music. So Wolfgang's only chance of success was to get himself known in as many places as possible, developing a reputation in foreign countries so as to gain recognition and respect at home. Leopold was far-sighted enough to understand that Salzburg was but

Carl Friedrich Abel was a
pioneer of public concerts.
His compositions, especially
his symphonies, greatly
influenced Mozart as a child
in London. (Gainsborough)

a dot on the map, and that the best jobs were to be found elsewhere.

When the family was heading back to Salzburg, via Switzerland, on that first three-and-a-half-year tour, Leopold wrote in a letter:

My children are used to work; if they became used to idleness on the excuse that this or that prevents their getting on with their tasks, the structure I have built would collapse. Habit is an iron shirt. But who knows what will happen when we get home to Salzburg? Perhaps we shall have such a reception that we shall gladly hoist our luggage on our backs and set off again. However, I am bringing my children back to their native land, God willing. If they are not wanted, I am not to blame. But they are not going to be had for nothing.

(From A. Hutchings, *Mozart*)

On the surface this reads like the demented ambitions of a tyrannical father, ruthlessly driving his children at the expense of a secure home life, endangering their health to fulfil a parental dream. That is why they put up with the endless jolting journeys in stage-coaches and carriages, the late nights hanging around in antechambers, waiting for an audience with some minor dignitary or flunkey who might put in a good word with a neighbouring prince. It was a high price to pay but Leopold saw it as the only avenue to success for Wolfgang, 'this miracle . . . which God let be born in Salzburg' as Leopold called him. 'I owe this to Almighty God, otherwise I should be a most thankless creature,' he wrote in a letter of 30 July 1768, when Wolfgang was twelve years old. 'And if it is ever to be my duty to convince the world of this miracle, it is so now, when people are ridiculing whatever is called miracle and are denying all miracles. Therefore they must be convinced.' To this end, Leopold served as Wolfgang's teacher, private secretary, road manager, valet, agent, publicist, impresario, copyist and proof-reader – everything the boy needed to embark on a career. In an age when scientists and free-thinkers were – to a conservative like Leopold – a dangerous threat to religion itself, Leopold saw his son as tangible proof of God's existence.

In London in June 1765 the Royal Society – the hallowed and impeccable centre of scientific truth – was called in to examine the eight-and-a-half-year-old Wolfgang. Daines Barrington, scholar, lawyer, philosopher and magistrate, was asked to scrutinise him and to write a detailed, learned account, later published in the *Philosophical Transactions of the Royal Society*. Their tests were rigorous: Leopold had said he was prepared for Wolfgang to be examined by any scientist they chose. As proof of his age, a copy of the boy's birth certificate was obtained from Salzburg. Wolfgang was asked to sight-read a five-line orchestral score of an operatic duet, playing from the manuscript, and at the same time to sing one of the vocal lines – which he did faultlessly. 'His father, who took the under part in the duet, was once or twice out . . . on which occasions the son looked back with some anger, pointing out to him his mistakes.' Daines Barrington then asked if young Wolfgang might improvise for him, but Leopold shook his head. Surely no further proof was required. Wolfgang, however, was happy to oblige and so Daines Barrington suggested he make up a love song. 'At this the boy looked back with much archness, and immediately began five or six lines of a jargon recitative proper to

The Honourable Daines Barrington, who examined Mozart's musical talent in London.

introduce a love song.' He then improvised an orchestral interlude and then he was asked to make up a 'Song of Rage'. This he did, 'and in the middle of it he had worked himself up into such a pitch, that he beat his harpsichord like a person possessed, sometimes rising in his chair. The word he pitched upon for this second extemporary composition was *perfido*.' After this he played a difficult keyboard piece, brilliantly, 'considering that his little fingers could scarcely span a fifth on the harpsichord. His astonishing readiness, however, did not arise merely from great practice; he had a thorough knowledge of the principles of composition, and was also a great master of modulations.' The session with Daines Barrington came to a charming conclusion when a kitten appeared and Wolfgang immediately got down from the harpsichord to play with it. 'Nor could we bring him back for a considerable time. He would also sometimes run about the room with a stick between his legs, by way of a horse. . .'

Inevitably, by the time he was in his teens, Wolfgang had become thoroughly accustomed to the flattery and adulation that had surrounded him all his life; and Leopold, too, had become used to hob-nobbing with aristocracy. Throughout, Leopold had been determined to better his social status, and his son had inherited some of these aspirations. Increasingly Wolfgang's letters contained an element of snobbishness, perhaps the inevitable result of being treated as an object of wonder by the crowned heads of Europe. In Italy the Pope himself had conferred upon Wolfgang the Order of the Golden Spur; yet at home in Salzburg the only regular job he could look forward to was with his father's employer, Colloredo, recently appointed Prince-Archbishop. (It is a misleading title because Colloredo's function, or perhaps the way he interpreted it, was largely administrative – a high-ranking civil servant, despite his elevated status as ruler of the principality.)

Wolfgang was formally taken on to the Archbishop's payroll at the age of sixteen as Konzertmeister, although he had held the post in an honorary capacity for three years. It was by no means an inferior appointment, but it was not as elevated as his father hoped for. However, the Salzburg job allowed time for Wolfgang to travel and compose music for other patrons – a concession he exploited to the full. Leopold hoped that Wolfgang would be offered a top job with the rank of Kapellmeister in a grand court with its own opera-house – possibly with the Archduke Ferdinand, son of the Empress Maria Theresa. She had been impressed by the music Wolfgang had com-

Count Colloredo, the last Prince-Archbishop of Salzburg and Mozart's employer.

posed for her son's wedding in Milan. She showed her admiration by presenting him not simply with a fee, but also with a watch studded with jewels, carrying her portrait in enamels. But the job never materialised. Indeed, Leopold's hard work tramping around Europe seems to have been counter-productive, because Maria Theresa wrote to her son advising him against employing such a composer 'or other useless people who run around the world like beggars'. So, for a time, both Leopold and Wolfgang had to be content with their lot in Salzburg and put up with Colloredo.

Colloredo was not a popular figure, possibly because he reduced public holidays by cutting down the number of official saints' days. Nor was he liked for his 'enlightened' views, or for keeping a portrait of Voltaire on the wall of his study. He changed the curriculum in schools to include philosophy and science, and he cut out much of the ceremonial of church services – which deeply offended the people of Salzburg. Moreover, he issued orders that mass, even on saints' days, should never exceed forty-five minutes. He pruned unnecessary expense and urged his employees to make economies, raise standards and generally look to their laurels.

This is not to say that he treated either Wolfgang or Leopold unfairly. On the contrary Colloredo was a violinist himself and claimed that all the best musicians came from Italy – an opinion shared at the time by many dignitaries in Germany and France. He accepted that Wolfgang was a musician of great talent, and that Leopold was an acknowledged expert on violin playing and the author of a highly-regarded textbook. But he placed father and son in exactly the same category as he did all his other employees: they were his servants, like his ostlers, his footmen, his kitchen staff, his gardeners and all the rest of his retinue. Leopold, on the other hand, had never seen himself like this and always felt that Wolfgang's God-given genius fitted him for better things. Wolfgang's salary as Konzertmeister was 150 florins – a reasonable wage for a sixteen-year-old, albeit an industrious and vastly talented one, as Colloredo would have been the first to admit. The friction that later developed between them stemmed from the fact that Colloredo – who by his own standards and by the standards of his day was not an unreasonable or intolerant man – simply could not accept that the Mozarts were getting ideas above their station.

Although he subsequently treated Mozart shabbily, Colloredo had little reason at first to complain about Wolfgang's behaviour, nor about the quality of the music he was composing. In addition to the church music required as part of his job, Mozart also wrote serenades, violin concertos and some of his loveliest piano concertos at this time. But matters came to a head within a few years. In March 1777 Wolfgang applied for permission to leave Salzburg with his father for yet another concert tour. Colloredo turned him down for the good reason that the Emperor was likely to visit Salzburg later in the summer; naturally, Wolfgang would be needed to supply the music expected of him for such an important occasion. In August Wolfgang tried again, writing an impassioned letter which stated pointedly that 'three years ago, when I asked permission to travel to Vienna, Your Grace himself declared that I had nothing to expect here, and would do better to seek my fortune elsewhere'. Colloredo agreed to let Wolfgang go, but Leopold remained in Salzburg. This time Wolfgang's mother accompanied her twenty-one-year-old son on his travels, and the family kept in touch, as was their habit, with letters to and from Salzburg.

However, when he arrived in Munich Wolfgang was treated as one who had broken ranks – a deserter. Nobody would give him a job for fear of offending Colloredo. In Mannheim, where he dearly wanted to be offered a post, he at least came into contact with the finest musicians from Austria and Bohemia, attracted to the Palatine court of Karl Theodor. At times the letters he sent to his father back in Salzburg smacked of arrogance. Leopold fretted, not unreasonably, afraid that Wolfgang's outspoken and indiscreet turn of phrase – in calling Colloredo, for example, 'an old prick' – would bring disaster.

In Mannheim Wolfgang met the Weber family and fell madly in love with Aloysia, the sixteen-year-old daughter and a more than capable singer. The Webers were, to say the least, a somewhat 'Bohemian' household who had come down in the world. They were spongers and Leopold had no wish for his son to be involved with such a family of tarts and wastrels, as he regarded them. In a sad and desperate outburst, we see Leopold – now aged fifty-six, his own career never truly fulfilled – suddenly aware that his son, a child no longer, is slipping away from him, headstrong and impetuous:

My dear son,

I read your letter of the 4th with surprise and horror. I am answering it today, the 11th, because I have been unable to sleep and am so tired out that I have to write slowly, word by word. If I am to finish by tomorrow, I should not recognise my son in that letter but for his familiar fault; he takes everybody at his word, opens his soft heart to flattery and fine speeches, lets everyone influence him in all directions and is so led away by sudden ideas and illusory visions that he is ready to fling his own reputation and profit to the winds, and even the interests of his old and honourable parents and his duty to them.

Gone are those happy hours when you would not go to sleep without first standing on a chair and singing to me, then kissing the end of my nose and saying that when I grow old you would put me in a glass case with a lid to protect me from the wind, and would always have me with you and honour me! Listen, therefore, patiently to me. You know our woes in Salzburg. You know my wretched salary, and you know why I kept my promise to let you go on your travels. You are aware of all my miseries.

There were two basic purposes for your journey: either to seek a permanent and good appointment, or, if that failed, to move forward to some place where there were prospects of big earnings. It depends on you alone to raise yourself to a greater eminence than any other musician has ever attained. You owe that to the extraordinary talents you have received from a most merciful God, and it depends only upon your own wisdom and behaviour whether you want to die as a mere musician forgotten by everyone, or as a famous Kapellmeister of whom posterity will read; whether, lulled to inertia by some woman, you die on a straw pallet in a room full of starving children or, after a Christian life of happiness, honour and fame, you pass away with your family well provided for and everybody respecting you.

(From A. Hutchings, Mozart)

Wolfgang's natural temperament was affectionate and generous. He was neither a wastrel nor a spendthrift, but simply hopeless with money. Leopold had devoted his life to promoting his son's career so that he might one day find a job that brought prestige and security. Now, an old man sitting at home in Salzburg, he was suddenly powerless, able no longer to chaperon, advise or control Wolfgang, or prevent him from becoming 'an easy touch'.

Wolfgang had failed to get a job in Munich and in Mannheim. He and his mother moved on to France. That summer of 1778 was to bring new and bitter frustrations. Mozart had hoped to teach the piano to wealthy and influential patrons, for which he would be generously rewarded, but he had little luck. On his first trip at the age of seven, the Parisian nobility had fawned over him and Wolfgang had snatched a kiss from the Marquise de Pompadour when she dandled him on her knee. Now, at twenty-two, and after travelling to Paris through the bitter cold March weather, he and his mother were reduced to living in one room with two beds, in a garret above a dealer in scrap metal. His mother was fifty-seven and the journey had exhausted her; she was, in fact, desperately ill:

I sit alone all day as if I were in prison. The room is dark and looks out on a closed, small yard. I can neither see the sun nor tell what the weather is. By great effort I can knit by the poor light. And for this we have to pay thirty livres a month! The door and stairs are so narrow that it would be impossible to get a piano up here. Wolfgang has to go out to M. Le Gros's house where there is a piano, and so I do not see him all the day. I shall soon forget how to talk.

(From A. Hutchings, Mozart)

Wolfgang trudged through the streets, which he found filthy, from one side of Paris to the other, soliciting for pupils, hoping to bring in a little money, but without much success: 'They say, "Oh, c'est un prodige, c'est inconcevable, c'est étonnant". Then it is goodbye.

At first I spent a good deal of time and money running round to them, often to find nobody at home.' He wrote his Concerto for Flute and Harp for the Duc de Guines and his daughter to play: 'She is a stupid and lazy girl and has not an idea in her head.' The Duke was slow in paying for the work. He and his mother found better accommodation, but by then her health had deteriorated and she died on 3 July.

Melchior Grimm, a family friend who had helped promote Mozart's original visit to Paris, wrote a letter to Leopold a few weeks after the death of Anna Maria Mozart:

Wolfgang is too generous, not pushy enough, too easily deceived, too little occupied with the means that lead to his fortune. To make headway in this place you need to be crafty, enterprising and bold. For his own sake I wish he had half the talent and twice the social conniving. . . . There are only two ways of getting on in this place. The first is to give piano lessons. Apart from the fact that one cannot secure pupils unless one actively tries, even by being a bit of a showman, I doubt if his health would stand the rigours of such an occupation, for it is extremely tiring to run to the four corners of Paris; besides, it would keep him from composition which is what is dearest to his heart.

(From A. Hutchings, *Mozart*)

Though Wolfgang was offered a post as organist at Versailles, he turned it down; perhaps he saw no future working in an atmosphere so full of intrigue; and therefore he had no option but to go back to Salzburg, his mother dead and his hopes of finding a suitable post shattered.

On 7 August he wrote to a friend:

You know quite well how I detest Salzburg, and not only because of the injustices which my dear father and I have endured there, which would be enough to make us want to forget the place and put it out of our thoughts for ever. But, overcoming that wish, if only we could manage our affairs to live there respectably! To live respectably and to live happily are very different matters; to do the latter in Salzburg I should need recourse to witchcraft. I have far more hope of living happily in any other place. Perhaps you will mistake me as supposing that Salzburg is too small for me? If so, you are quite wrong.

(From A. Hutchings, *Mozart*)

Wolfgang's dissatisfaction with Salzburg had not stemmed solely from his dislike of Colloredo; he was equally concerned that there was no opera-house and that standards of singing and orchestral playing were low. But in his absence several key posts had become vacant due to the deaths of the Salzburg court organist and the Kapellmeister. As far as Leopold was concerned, Wolfgang and he could take over the double responsibility which would totally change their fortunes. Leopold spread across Salzburg the rumour that his son had enjoyed quite extraordinary success in Paris. In due course the word got back to Colloredo who, for his part, let it be known that he felt no ill-will towards Wolfgang and that his return, far from being a humiliation, would be welcomed. Indeed, in his belief that a musician should hear fresh works from time to time, Colloredo was quite happy for a form of contract whereby Wolfgang could travel to Italy every alternate year and could take time away from Salzburg to fulfil opera commissions.

Wolfgang did not hurry back to Salzburg, hoping Colloredo would imagine that his services were in great demand en route: 'Please, dearest father, make use of this news in Salzburg. Talk about it so often and so emphatically that the Archbishop may suppose I shall not return; he may then decide to offer a better stipend,' he wrote. The duplicity, if only for the time being, enabled Wolfgang to return, with at least some dignity, on 17 January 1779, to serve the Archbishop as Konzertmeister and organist.

The flash-point was reached at the end of the following year. At the beginning of November 1780, Wolfgang left for Munich to complete his opera *Idomeneo* and to prepare for the first orchestral rehearsal on 1 December. Colloredo had granted him six weeks' leave of absence. Nannerl and Leopold joined him in Munich in time for the first dress rehearsal on 27 January, Wolfgang's birthday. The première of *Idomeneo* two days later was a triumphant success. Afterwards Wolfgang relaxed for it was carnival time in Munich. He had a riotous time: '. . . that was youthful folly, for I thought "Where will you be after this? Back in Salzburg! Enjoy yourself while you can".'

When six weeks' leave had stretched to four months, Wolfgang was summoned to join Colloredo in Vienna, one of the centres of the musical world, along with the other Salzburg musicians. Although we have only Wolfgang's one-sided account, it is clear that Colloredo had decided to cut him down to size once and for all. Treated not as a great composer but as a lackey, Wolfgang complained that he was made to eat with the hoi polloi; the food, he said, was abominable. (But since he ate at the same table as the cooks, that could be an exaggeration – kitchen staff have ways of not stinting themselves.) What he really objected to was being placed amongst the servants. 'Stupid, coarse jokes are made,' he wrote, 'but not with me; for if I have to speak at all I do so with the utmost gravity, and leave as soon as

I have finished. At night we do not feed together, but each man receives three ducats, which is a relief.'

More serious, though, was the way Colloredo brought him to heel, treating him as a rank-and-file musician. In the evening it was part of a musician's job to wait on call in an antechamber until required. In due course, a flunkey would summon the musicians into the salon to provide entertainment for the prince and his guests. To Wolfgang this was an insult – even though he was paid for his trouble. Colloredo, moreover, insisted that Wolfgang should stay in attendance on evenings when – as Colloredo well knew – Mozart would have to turn down other, more lucrative, engagements:

The Archbishop enjoys a reputation for goodness and the honour his servants win for him, and then robs them of their earnings while paying them nothing himself. I shall wait and see if I get no money, and if I am not paid I shall go to the Archbishop and tell him plainly that he must pay me if I may not earn outside.

(From A. Hutchings, *Mozart*)

For Wolfgang this was intolerable. There, in Vienna, he calculated, he could earn more in a couple of months than he could in a year at Salzburg.

He was asked to take part in a charity concert in aid of widows and orphans on 3 April at the Kärntnertor Theatre. All the best musicians in the city were providing their services free. At first Colloredo refused to allow him, but in the end Wolfgang got his own way. It was his first public appearance in Vienna and he was a great success. One of the works was his Symphony No. 36 in C Major. The standard of the orchestral playing was superb. But the greatest acclaim was for his piano playing, so persistent that he 'had to start all over again because the applause would not stop'.

Wolfgang was determined to stay in Vienna and wrote home to his father telling him so. Leopold was anxious, fearing his own job might also be in jeopardy. Much to Colloredo's credit, he seems never to have blamed Leopold, but, in a final humiliation, he summoned Wolfgang, insisting that the composer return with him to Salzburg carrying 'an important parcel'. Since all the rest of Archbishop Colloredo's musicians were also making the trip, there seems no reason for his insistence except to insult Wolfgang. He refused to act as messenger-boy, and on 9 May Colloredo accused him of insolence:

. . . It all came out in one breath; that I was the most disorderly fellow he knew, that nobody else served him so badly, and that if I did not leave him today he would write home to get my stipend stopped. I had no chance to get a word in for he raged on like a fire. He lied to my face, saying that my salary was 500 gulden, called me a rogue, villain, and conceited fool. Indeed I should not like to put it all down in writing. Finally my blood rose to boiling and I said: 'Isn't your Grace satisfied with me?' 'What, do you dare to threaten, you fool? Oh, you conceited fool. There's the door; I'll have no more to do with such a wretched scoundrel.' Finally I said: 'Nor will I have anything more to do with you. You will have it in writing tomorrow.'

You are quite wrong [Wolfgang told his father] if you fancy that the nobility and the Emperor will think the less of me for this. The Archbishop is hated here, most of all by the Emperor. That is the real reason for his temper. Now my good fortune is beginning, and I hope that it will also be yours. Write to me in code and tell me that you are pleased, for indeed so you ought to be. But condemn me in public, so that nobody will think that you are responsible. If the Archbishop shows you the slightest insult, bring my sister and join me immediately in Vienna. I can assure you on my honour that all three of us can make a living here. Yet the wisest course would be to endure another year. Do not send any more letters to the Deutsches Haus [Colloredo's Viennese residence].

(From A. Hutchings, *Mozart*)

Leopold was horrified and tried to intervene by seeking the help of Count Arco, another member of Colloredo's retinue, who had always been a good friend. On 10 May when Wolfgang tried to hand in his resignation, Count Arco refused to accept it, saying that Wolfgang should remember his obligation towards his father: 'I assured him at once that I knew my duty to my father as well as he did, perhaps better', wrote Wolfgang. The following week there was another meeting with Count Arco who again attempted to calm Wolfgang's impulsiveness:

'Believe me [he said], you are letting yourself be dazzled here. A man's fame does not last long in Vienna. At first you may hear nothing but praise, and earn a good deal of money, but for how long? After a few months the Viennese want novelty. . .'

'It is the Archbishop's fault, not mine [replied Wolfgang], that this has happened in Vienna. If he knew how to treat men of talent it would not have happened. Count Arco, I am the most amiable person in the world, provided that people are the same with me.'

'Well,' he said, 'the Archbishop thinks you insufferably insolent' . . .

'Certainly I am towards him, for I do to others as they do to me. When I perceive that someone insults and belittles me I can be as proud as a peacock.'

Amongst other things he asked if I did not suppose that he also had frequently to swallow harsh words. I shrugged my shoulders and answered: 'You must have your reasons for tolerating them; I have mine for not doing so.'

(From A. Hutchings, *Mozart*)

Six days later, having done everything possible to settle matters amicably, Count Arco finally lost his temper with Wolfgang and kicked him out. Wolfgang wrote:

So this is the way to win people over, to soften them up! By refusing from innate stupidity to accept petitions, by not daring to say anything to one's master from cowardice and sycophancy, to keep one on tenterhooks for a month and finally, when one is forced to present the petition, throwing one out of the door with a kick up the behind. That's the style!

(From A. Hutchings, *Mozart*)

For Leopold, now aged sixty-one, this was the end of his dreams, and in all probability the end of his own career, for his son's letters now threatened revenge:

I shall soon write to the Count telling him what he can expect from me as soon as I am lucky enough to meet him again – never mind where – provided it is no place where I must show him respect. Keep my stick and carry it all the time. Who knows whether in your hands it might not avenge its former owner upon Arco? The heart ennobles a man. Although I am not a count, I have more honour in my heart than many a count. Lackey or count, whoever insults me is treated by me as a rascal.

(From A. Hutchings, *Mozart*)

In time the matter fizzled out. Wolfgang never carried out his threat of physical violence, and Colloredo does not appear to have victimised Leopold for his son's behaviour.

At first, Wolfgang did well in Vienna, where he lodged with the Webers, falling in love with, and subsequently marrying, Constanze after his first love, her sister Aloysia, had married the actor and painter Joseph Lange. He found that he was earning good money, often for curious reasons. On Christmas Eve 1781 he was engaged in a piano-playing contest with the brilliant pianist Muzio Clementi. Clementi, it was said, displayed superior technical skill, but Mozart's playing was regarded as more musicianly. The result was an 'honourable draw' and Mozart was extremely satisfied with the fee he received – 'more than half my annual Salzburg salary'.

Keyboard battles, similar to the 'cuttin' contests' between jazz pianists, were popular in the eighteenth and nineteenth centuries, with one player attempting to outshine his rival. Moreover, to Mozart and his contemporaries, the piano was still a modern sound with its potential for an expressive, singing legato – the notes of a musical phrase joined smoothly together. The instrument at that stage lacked the massive iron-framed sonority that became possible during the nineteenth century, but it could still produce a resonant fortissimo and a delicate pianissimo and a wide range of tone-colours in between, impossible to achieve on the harpsichord. At the end of his life J. S. Bach had encountered the early, and by no means perfect, Silbermann pianos. He was not overimpressed by the invention, but even he had to admit that it offered considerable subtlety of expression and – to translate his comment into today's phraseology – would sort out the real musicians from the keyboard cowboys. The young Beethoven, soon to impress the Viennese with his playing, was also involved in such piano contests. Later in the nineteenth century other great lions of the keyboard did battle together – Franz Liszt and Sigismond Thalberg for instance – at a time when the modern concert grand was becoming an established fact of musical life.

In its way, the contest between Wolfgang Mozart and Muzio Clementi must have been no less impressive. Clementi was a brilliant virtuoso who had delighted London's musical public with his rapid scales and elaborate trills. Mozart, on the other hand, was never looked on in that light by his contemporaries. Present on that occasion was the composer Carl Ditters von Dittersdorf, who later recounted his impressions to the Emperor Joseph II, and noted their conversation:

Emperor: Have you heard Mozart play?
Dittersdorf: Three times so far.
Emperor: What do you think of him?
Dittersdorf: As any connoisseur must, I admire him.
Emperor: Have you heard Clementi?
Dittersdorf: Yes I have.
Emperor: Some people put him above Mozart, amongst them Bigwig [the nick-name for Kreibich, director of the imperial orchestra]. What do you say? Be quick and frank about it.
Dittersdorf: Clementi plays with art: Mozart plays with art *and* taste.
Emperor: That is exactly what I said.

Mozart, rather uncharitably, dismissed Clementi as 'a mere *mechanicus*', but Clementi was much more generous in his response to Mozart, whose playing, he said, was overwhelming; in the songlike slow movements in particular he had 'never before heard anyone play with such intelligence and grace'.

Wolfgang greatly admired the quality of pianos to be found in Vienna and, in those early years there, he attracted wealthy pupils, some of whom were genuinely talented. He made friends with influential families and raised his charges for piano tuition: 'I no longer charge for twelve lessons, but by the month, having learnt to my cost that the ladies often miss their lessons for weeks at a time. Now they will have to pay six ducats whether they use me or not.'

However, the fickleness of the Viennese public came as a bitter disappointment to Mozart; there were many aristocrats around who could easily have helped him financially or introduced him to wealthy patrons. The freelance existence that he lived in his last ten years was to be harrowing and tragic, and a bitter contrast with the success Haydn enjoyed, especially towards the end of his life. The two men were close friends. Despite the twenty-five years' age difference, they respected each other professionally, to the point where they directly influenced each other.

Haydn's composing technique was well developed before he came into contact with the musical tastes of foreign countries. Mozart, on the other hand, as we have seen, was an itinerant musician from childhood, thoroughly versed in national differences and prevailing fashions. But that explains only part of his genius. He brought to the Classical symphony not only depths of expression, but the idea that the musical phrase is inextricably bound up with the particular coloration of the instrument that plays it – the clarinet, for example – and the way those tone-colours subtly change from low notes to high. He understood too how gradations of phrasing and 'attack' and the nature of the instrument itself must, in the end, dictate the sort of music written for it – that oboists need to snatch a breath, for instance – and that an infinite range of shading is possible when music 'lies well' on an instrument.

Ultimately inexplicable are Mozart's innate sense of balance and symmetry, where one musical phrase is mirrored by another, his unparalleled gift of melody, and his extraordinary rhythmic vocabulary – the underlying thrust of his music, infinitely subtle and flexible, not just from moment to moment but throughout the entire span of a complete work, often composed to an impossibly pressing deadline. The 'Haffner' Symphony (No. 35), for instance, was written straight off, first page to last, and despatched movement by movement. When he received a copy in Vienna six months later, Wolfgang wrote to his father saying, 'My new "Haffner" Symphony has positively amazed me, for I had forgotten every single note of it!' Similarly, his 'Linz' Symphony (No. 36) was composed in a matter of days, but the work gives not the slightest impression of haste. Neither do his last three symphonies, completed in six and a half weeks in the summer

The first page of Mozart's Symphony No. 41 in C, the 'Jupiter', the last of his three great symphonies composed in the summer of 1788.

of 1788, at the bleakest time of his life. He and his wife were in Vienna, desperately poor and moving house yet again. He had to write begging letters just to stay alive. Their six-month-old daughter Theresa was dying of dysentery (all but two of Mozart's six children died within six months of birth). Yet in the midst of all this, between 26 June and 10 August, he was able to complete three of the finest symphonies ever written, each one different in its diversity of expression. No. 39 in E Flat is serene and joyous, with almost the feeling of chamber music in the delight and interplay of themes. No. 40 in G Minor is different again, dominated by a passionate, rhythmic impetus. While his last symphony, No. 41 in C, the 'Jupiter', is different again – a work of enormous power that culminates in a technical *tour de force* – 'perfect, as if created by God' was Grieg's description.

In the richness and diversity of these three symphonies, Mozart transcended the agony and the despair of his day-to-day circumstances – a summer blighted by poverty and sorrow, enough to choke any thought of creativity. Yet the ultimate mystery is how the music of Mozart defies description. He can make us happy and sad, jubilant and reflective, and all at the same time. No other composer has that gift. How was this possible? Was it callous detachment that enabled him to go on working with his baby daughter dying in the next room?

In the works of many other composers — Berlioz, Tchaikovsky, Richard Strauss, for example — music sometimes expressed personal events: a diary of distress and elation. But to a Classical composer, and to Mozart in particular, such a thing was impossible. He saw music, as these last three symphonies and indeed all his music demonstrate so abundantly, as a quest for beauty. He once said, 'Music must never offend the ear, but must please the hearer or, in other words, must never cease to be music.'

In the world of Beethoven and his successors, all that was to change; the expressive imperative of the artist would soon stretch and shatter such a philosophy. When Mozart died in 1791, three and a half years after writing those last three symphonies, Haydn said of him: 'The world will not see such a talent again. Friends flatter me that I have some genius, but he stood far above me.'

That is a remarkable tribute from one composer to another, even from Haydn, a most kind and generous personality. But as a fellow musician Haydn could see how, within the lifespan of thirty-five years, Mozart produced an enormous number of operas, concertos, symphonies, chamber music, keyboard and church music, each a magnificent expression of the human spirit.

We have looked at some of the influences that contributed towards Mozart's musical personality. We have seen the contacts he made, from the age of six, with musicians and composers in Mannheim, Paris, London, Italy and elsewhere. And we have seen how, by his mid-teens, all this wealth of experience had been absorbed into a fully mature, creative artist. Where did all this creativity come from? How could it all be compressed into one man, blue eyes, light brown hair, five foot four? We can attribute a great deal to natural ability and a talent inherited from Leopold, who was certainly an excellent teacher. But the same could be said for many other composers, none of them in the same league as Mozart.

Where, then, do we look? The quickest and perhaps the ultimate explanation is to consider one of his Christian names — Theophilus. It comes from the Greek, but Mozart preferred its Latin version, Amadeus. It has been translated as 'loving God'. Mozart's talent was a gift in return.

3

'A Little Place in the Country'

Poverty and hardship blighted the last years of Mozart's life although there were many influential people in Vienna who could easily have helped him towards secure employment but chose not to. Nobody doubted his talent. Nobody could overlook the obvious fact that this young man in his early thirties was an opera composer of real genius. Was not everybody humming *Figaro*? Yet he was not popular with the fickle Viennese, and Leopold's dream that one day his son would land a job as Kapellmeister, where he would have control of an opera-house and a resident orchestra, was never realised. For Joseph Haydn, however, that was exactly what happened when he joined the staff of the Esterházy family, the richest in Hungary.

Prince Nikolaus Esterházy 'the Magnificent' planned regular opera seasons at his palace, a former hunting lodge set in the marshes at the edge of a lake in the west of the country and transformed by the Esterházy family into a permanent summer residence intended to rival Versailles. The palace boasted its own opera-house and marionette theatre, together with rehearsal rooms and apartments for singers and musicians. Haydn had a four-roomed suite. The public rooms were lavishly decorated. There were a fine library and a picture gallery, both set in spacious parklands. Opera librettos were printed and talent scouts, acting on behalf of the Prince, culled the best singers from Italy and sent back the scores of new operas. Some idea of the Prince's enthusiasm for opera can be gained from the number of performances that took place. In a single decade (between 1780 and 1790) there were 1038 opera performances, sixty-seven of which were premières. Although the orchestra never had more than two dozen players, it contained some fine musicians and the soloists in the opera productions were among the greatest singers in Europe. They were often engaged on short-term contracts, and those accustomed to the sunnier climes of Italy constantly complained about the harsh north wind from the lake and the damp and cold of the marshes.

Esterházy cost thirteen million gulden to build. Compare that to the 2000 gulden Haydn received in October 1778 when he sold the comfortable but little-used house he owned in Eisenstadt. The Palace

Joseph Haydn. Having dressed in his best clothes, Haydn would start his working day improvising at the keyboard before committing his musical ideas to paper.

— badly damaged during the 1939–45 war, but now lovingly restored as a tourist showpiece — contained 126 rooms. The first Prince Nikolaus, it was reported,

always divides a part of his entertainment with everyone. Whenever friends of some standing come to Esterházy and take up quarters in the *Gasthaus*, he sends his carriage, has them taken to his castle and invites them to dine with him. Every day there is theatre, three times a week Italian opera and the same for German plays. The entrance is free for everyone. When new pieces are given, he has the libretti printed in Oedenburg and distributed to the audience. His wish that in this magnificent castle there should always reign happiness and politeness, is followed explicitly by his personnel. Most rooms in the castle are designed for great rulers who from time to time come here. The Prince and dowager Princess live on the *rez-de-chaussée*. The Prince has some four hundred clocks, each one of different and beautiful workmanship. Among the most remarkable that I saw was one with a stuffed canary which every hour sings an aria like a real bird, and the beak, breast and the whole body move like a real bird; and there are various clocks with all sorts of music. A similar musical plaything is an armchair which, when you sit in it, begins to play various pieces and continues with new ones.

His chamber musicians wear a uniform (green coats with red and gold) and at their head is Haydn, a man whose music is admired in Italy, England and France.

(From H. C. Robbins Landon, Haydn, a documentary study,
Thames and Hudson, 1981)

Haydn's orchestra at Esterházy was small by modern standards. There was another major difference from the type of orchestra to which we are now accustomed: until very late in the eighteenth century, a harpsichordist, seated in the middle of the orchestra, played an important role. One of his tasks was to hold the performance together, the equivalent you might say of the modern musical director-conductor, still to be found in the orchestra pit of theatres today. The harpsichordist was frequently also the composer. His job was to fill in the harmony by improvising chords above a bass-line – the *basso continuo* or continuo for short. He would direct the performance from the keyboard, sharing the responsibility with the principal violinist, who stood at the front of the violin section and controlled the upper 'voices' of the orchestra. Today we would call him the leader or, in America, the concertmaster. A conductor, standing in front of the orchestra waving a stick, is a nineteenth-century invention.

The continuo player was particularly necessary in smaller establishments, where the payroll might be reduced suddenly, and players dismissed or called away on other duties. It would then be left to the harpsichordist to fill in the missing instrumental parts. Conversely, in wealthier, more secure establishments, there would be people, normally employed in the stables, who played hunting horns. From the barrack square came flutes, trumpets, kettledrums and bassoons. Later in the eighteenth century, as they became more reliable, clarinets were available. In this way, the Classical, pre-Beethoven orchestra – the foundation of the modern symphony orchestra – developed not so much from some idealised quest for the right sound, as from sheer practicality – whichever employees might be spared from the chase or from the drill sergeant.

Writing symphonies was part of Haydn's regular job at Esterházy. Symphonic composition spanned forty years of his life and his works

Prince Nikolaus Esterházy 'the Magnificent'.

Haydn taking part in a string quartet. (Hanfstengel after Julius Schmid)

encompass an abundance of stylistic features. Although he established the string quartet, he is also justifiably called 'the father of the symphony'. By the 1760s, when he went to Esterházy, the symphony had already moved well away from its origins in the operatic overture – the *sinfonia avanti l'opera*, the short, three-section piece that silenced the chatter of latecomers and indicated that something splendid was about to happen. And so the 'symphony', as an independent work for orchestra, was increasingly regarded as a vehicle for a composer's skill and powers of expression, with more organised musical material than the string of dance movements found in orchestral suites. Haydn was expected to produce music at speed for all types of occasions; creativity was followed by instant assessment, which meant he could experiment with all sorts of novel effects. Indeed, Haydn often said that the remoteness of Esterházy, tucked away in the Hungarian countryside, forced him to produce original work:

My prince was satisfied with all my works. I was praised. As head of an orchestra, I could experiment, observe what heightened the effect and what weakened it, and so could improve, expand, cut, take risks. I was cut off from the world; there was no one near me to bother me or make me doubt myself, so I had to become original.

(From H. C. Robbins Landon, *Haydn*)

Haydn, who was a delightful fellow, revelled in the chance to try out new musical tricks. His most endearing quality is his bountiful, knockabout sense of humour. When he is serious, he is never ponderous. In the midst of a solemn, straight-faced section, he will suddenly wander off into unrelated keys, for no other reason than pure fun. Other eighteenth-century composers will balance their phrases with immaculate orthodoxy: two plus two; or four bars balanced by another four. Haydn, on the other hand, loves to spring at you suddenly with an irregular phrase of seven or eleven bars, stretching or compressing the cadence you have come to expect – the musical equivalent of climbing down a ladder, only to discover the bottom rung is missing. He treats his musical phrases not as self-sufficient entities, but as clauses in a paragraph. And he loves nothing more than to inject a sudden fortissimo on to a weak beat, and to catch you on the hop by hurling in a whole sequence of cross-rhythms – one of the tricks he is said to have picked up from Hungarian folk-music.

Haydn writes with particular players in mind, tailoring the music to their capabilities and personalities. He is also concerned that his audience should have a good time too, and solicits applause by cramming his finales with plenty of good tunes, underpinned by a brisk, rhythmic drive carried through with high spirits. Such finales make his symphonies genuinely attractive – one of the reasons why Haydn was for so long regarded as good old genial 'Papa Haydn'.

When a symphony ends with a few pages of unbridled good humour, we tend to forget the emotional depths and the intellectual control of earlier movements. But these qualities are all finely judged in Haydn's mature symphonies, the six he composed for Paris in 1785 and the twelve he wrote for his two visits to London a few years later, when he was a grand old man in his early sixties and the toast of the town.

It was Johann Peter Salomon who for a handsome sum commissioned Haydn to come to London. He was a shrewd and lavish operator: impresario, skilled violinist and composer. But his greatest talent was his ability to make things happen, coupled with a breadth of vision and a canny understanding of the tastes of London audiences. German-born, he settled in England and came to dominate the capital's musical life, establishing his reputation first as a violinist and subsequently as a concert promoter.

In September 1790 the musical glories of Esterházy stopped

abruptly with the death of Haydn's patron, Prince Nikolaus. During his lifetime, Haydn served four princes of the Esterházy family and for many years was happy enough, saying that the Palace of Esterházy was a place 'where I should like to live and die'. Though the court musicians were paid off, Haydn was left a generous pension by Nikolaus (1000 gulden per year) in recognition of his devoted service. However, one of the first actions of Prince Anton – the new head of the family – was to get rid of the musical entourage and close the opera-house. Haydn left for Vienna.

By chance, Salomon was in Cologne on one of his regular talent-spotting trips to Europe to sign up singers for his next season of London concerts. Typically, the moment he heard of the death of Prince Nikolaus he headed for Vienna. According to Haydn's contemporary and biographer, Albert Christoph Dies, Salomon – clearly a man who came straight to the point – greeted Haydn with: 'I am Salomon of London and have come to fetch you. Tomorrow we will arrange an *accord*.' Salomon achieved his ambition and they struck a deal; Haydn was contracted on the generous terms of 5000 gulden for the year to give concerts in London. Salomon wanted him to go immediately to England, but the fifty-eight-year-old composer was initially apprehensive about taking on the commission. He was, after all, no longer a young man and it was a hazardous journey in the depths of winter through a Europe in political turmoil. However, Salomon persisted and Haydn agreed. But he wished first to bid farewell to a dear friend, Wolfgang Amadeus Mozart.

Haydn's admiration and affection for Mozart can be gauged from part of a letter he wrote three years earlier, in December 1787, to Franz Rott of Prague, who had hoped to commission a composition from Haydn:

You ask me for an *opera buffa*. Scarcely any man can brook comparison with the great Mozart. If I could only impress on the soul of every friend of music, on high personages in particular, how inimitable are Mozart's works, how profound, how musically intelligent, how extraordinarily sensitive! (for this is how I understand them, how I feel them) – why then the nations would vie with each other to possess such a jewel within their frontiers. Prague should hold him fast – but should reward him too; for without this, the history of great geniuses is sad indeed, and gives but little encouragement to posterity to further exertions; and unfortunately this is why so many promising intellects fall by the wayside. It enrages me to think that this incomparable Mozart is not yet engaged by some imperial or royal court! Forgive me if I lose my head: but I love the man so dearly.

(From H. C. Robbins Landon, *Haydn*)

Haydn introduced Salomon to Mozart in Vienna just before Christmas, and Mozart tried to talk Haydn out of going to England, as Georg Griesinger, Haydn's biographer and confidant, reported: 'Mozart said, at a merry meal with Salomon, to Haydn: "You won't stand it for long and will soon return, for you aren't young any more." "But I am still vigorous and in good health," answered Haydn.' Dies adds, 'Mozart then pointed out to Haydn, calling him "Papa" as he always did: "You have had no education for the great world, and you speak too few languages." "Oh," replied Haydn, "my language is understood all over the world!"'

Haydn left Vienna with Salomon on 15 December 1790. According to Dies,

Mozart, that day, never left his friend Haydn. He dined with him, and at the moment of parting, he said, 'We are probably saying our last adieu in this life'. Tears welled in both their eyes. Haydn was deeply moved, for he applied Mozart's words to himself, and the possibility never occurred to him that the thread of Mozart's life could be cut by fate the very next year.

(From H. C. Robbins Landon, *Haydn*)

For Haydn it was the start of a glorious autumnal period when he produced many of his finest compositions. He arrived in England on New Year's Day, 1791, and from then on was treated as a celebrity, fêted wherever he went. His notebooks make lively reading:

My arrival caused a great sensation throughout the whole city, and I went the round of all the newspapers for 3 successive days. Everyone wants to know me. I had to dine out 6 times up to now, and if I wanted, I could dine out every day; but first I must consider my health, and 2nd my work. Except for the nobility, I admit no callers till 2 o'clock in the afternoon, and at 4 o'clock I dine at home with Mon. Salomon. I have nice and comfortable, but expensive, lodgings . . . but everything is expensive here.

(From H. C. Robbins Landon, *Haydn*)

Haydn adored London and all classes of society, but the size and noise bothered him: 'I wished I could fly for a time to Vienna, to have more quiet in which to work, for the noise that the common people make as they sell their wares in the street is intolerable.' Soon, he moved from his lodgings at 18 Great Pulteney Street, in the heart of Soho, to the pastoral calm of Lisson Grove in St John's Wood, at that time a small village in the rolling countryside a mile or so north of the fog and noise of London.

Haydn was an affable and charming man, always happy to stop and talk and pass the time of day with anybody of whatever station

A programme for a concert given by Haydn in Hanover Square in 1791.

HANOVER-SQUARE.

MR. HAYDN's NIGHT.

MAY the 16th, 1791.

PART THE FIRST.

New Grand Overture ———— HAYDN.

Aria ———— Signora STORACE.

Concertante for Two Corni Baffetti,
Meffrs. SPRINGER and DWORSACK.

New Aria, with Oboe and Baffoon obligati,
Signor DAVID.———— *Haydn.*

Concerto, Violin ———— Mr. GIORNOVICHI.

PART THE SECOND.

By particular Defire, the New G. and Overture, *Haydn,*
as performed at Mr. Salomon's firft Concert.

Cantata—Signor PACCHIEROTTI.———— *Haydn.*

Concertante for Piano Forte and Pedal Harp,
Mr. DUSSECK, and Madame KRUMPHOLTZ.

Duetto—Sig. DAVID and Sig. PACCHIEROTTI.

Finale ———— HAYDN.

RONDO. Signora STORACE.

Cimarofa.

INFELICE ch'io fono !
A tè diedi il mio core
Di tè mi fido, e tù m'inganni !
Oh Dio ! qual pena amara
Qual affanno è il mio
Mifera in tale ftato che mai far deggio
Porgerti la deftra farai viltà
Gl'affetti a un traditore
Pria di giurar, m'incenerifca amore.

Il mio cor, gl' affetti miei
A chi mai più donerò
Se crudel con me tù fei
Di chi fidarmi oh Dio non sò
Cari amici ... il cor vi lafcio ...
Tù rammenta ... ah fi crudele ...
Di queft' alma a tè fedele
Sentirai mà invan pietà
Son oppreffa dal deftino
Mi divora in fen l'affanno
Fiera forte amor tiranno
Perchè tanta crudeltà.

CANTATA. Signor PACCHIEROTTI.

RECIT. *Haydn.*

AH come il core mi palpita nel feno
Per Fillide infedel morì Fileno.
Omnipotenti Numi, che leffi !
Ah mia tiranna inumana pieta
Tu per falvarlo foffi l'empia cagion della fua morte,
Crudeliffima legge ingrata forte !
Ohime ! di fofco velo fi fcopre il giorno
Io gelo, il piè vacilla oh Dio !
Ombra dell' Idol mio, fra mirti degli Elifi
Il noftro amor fi eternerà frà poco
Teco farò ... Che fento ? ... Ah ! tu fdegnofa
Dal margine di lete mi rifpondi
Tra fofpiri funefti. Fuggi infida da me,
Tu mi uccidefti.

ARIA.

Ombra del caro bene
Ah non chiamarmi infida
Fidati a me, e fida
Verto frà la ombre ancor.
Tiranna a me ti refe
Una pieta fedele
Mi refe a te crudele
Un infelice amor.

ARIA. Signor DAVID.

Haydn.

CARA deh torna in pace
Non ti filegnar ben mio
Troppo m'affanno oh Dio
La pena del tuo cor.
Barbaro io vado a morte
Ah che l'affanno mio
Mi porta a delirar.

DUETTO.

Signor DAVID and Signor PACCHIEROTTI.

RECIT. *Bianchi.*

PADRE fon teco ;
Io della morte la via t' infegnerò

A. 2. Ho non la temo.
Cofi ci ferba o Ciel nel punto eftremo.

DUETTO.

Gual. Caro Padre a te vicino
Infelice io non fon più

Ermes. Figlio amato del deftino
Ta trionfa la virtù

A. 2. Già ritorna alfin queft' alma
A goder la dolce calma
Già ritorna à refpirar.

J. 8 - 360

Printed by H. REYNELL, (No. 21,) Piccadilly, near the Hay-Market.

in society. He was a great man for the ladies, admitting that his own unsatisfactory marriage to a rather shrewish woman made him therefore 'less indifferent to the charms of other women'. In London he met Mrs Schroeter, widow of the man who had succeeded Johann Christian Bach as Master of the King's Musick. 'Though already sixty years old,' Haydn said, 'she was still a beautiful and charming woman and I would have married her easily if I had been free at the time.' All Haydn's biographers confirm that the composer freely admitted that he could not understand how he had been loved by so many pretty women: 'They can't have been led to it by my beauty.' Haydn's London friends also included a sea captain, a banker, the Duchess of York, George III and other members of the ruling family and a 'Mr March – dentist, coachmaker and dealer in wines – a man 84 years old with a very young mistress'.

In the 1790s London was the musical capital of the world, with either the opera or an important concert to look forward to every night of the week. With so much socialising Haydn found it difficult to get down to work on the new pieces he had promised for Salomon's well-advertised series of twelve subscription concerts, scheduled for Friday evenings. A ticket for the series cost five guineas – and the advertisement in the press clearly anticipated chaos in Hanover Square. As a solution, a one-way traffic system was proposed: 'The subscribers are intreated to give particular orders to their Coachmen to set down and take up at the Side Door in the Street, with the Horses' Heads towards the Square.'

The opening concert was a great success, and the following day the *Morning Chronicle* stated: 'Never, perhaps, was there a richer musical treat.' The reviewer placed Haydn on the same level as the Bard himself, 'for like our own SHAKSPEARE [*sic*], he moves and governs the passions at his will'. We are left in no doubt whatever about Haydn's popularity: the reviewer was not in the least surprised 'that to souls capable of being touched by music, HAYDN should be an object of homage, and even of idolatry'. Dr Charles Burney recounted in his memoirs the thrill of attending these orchestral concerts: 'Haydn himself presided at the piano-forte; and the sight of that renowned composer so electrified the audience, as to excite an attention and a pleasure superior to any that had ever, to my knowledge, been caused by instrumental music in England.'

The orchestra in the concert rooms in Hanover Square was set out in a novel way. Haydn directed proceedings from the keyboard, sit-

Hypothetical reconstruction (by Neal Zaslaw, after contemporary sources) of the amphitheatre arrangement of the orchestra introduced to London by Haydn for the Salomon concerts of 1791–3: positions are indicated for the organ, chorus and soloists (although oratorios were not given at these concerts).

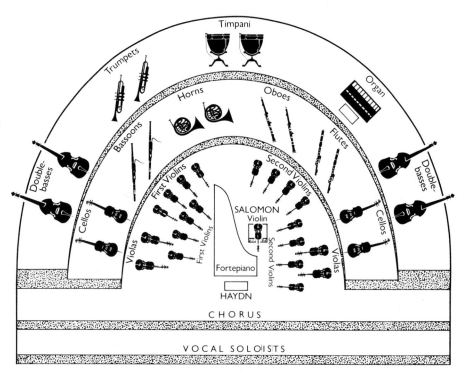

ting in the middle of the orchestra. Salomon, with violin, led the players standing at a music desk, raised up on a rostrum positioned at the side of the piano. These subscription concerts of 1791 were enormously popular and Haydn readily remained in England for another year. At Oxford he was bedecked in the magnificent gown of cream and pink silk when the university honoured him Doctor of Music. It was customary to wear the gown for three days after the ceremony, which caused Haydn on several occasions to quip in his rich Austrian accent: 'I would have dearly liked my Viennese acquaintances to see me in this dress!' He was, however, delighted by the whole affair. Always meticulous in financial dealings – he itemised the expenses in his pocket-book – he noted the trip cost him a total of six guineas which included half a guinea for the academic robe and one and a half guineas for the bells to be rung.

On 5 November he attended a lavish banquet in London's Guildhall, given in honour of the Lord Mayor and attended by 1200 notables, including the Lord Chancellor, the Duke of Leeds, William Pitt and the dignitaries and Aldermen of London. He noted that the food was 'very nice and well-cooked' with many kinds of wine in abundance, but the noise and heat of the occasion horrified him. He particularly disliked the dancing that followed – endless minuets, played 'by a wretched dance band, the entire orchestra consisting only of two violins and a violoncello. The minuets were more Polish than in our or the Italian manner.' After a quarter of an hour he could stand it no more and fled from the heat and the crush.

From there I went to another room, which was more like a subterranean cavern, and where the dance was English; the music was a little better because there was a drum in the band which drowned the misery of the violins. I went on to the great hall, where we had eaten, and there the band was larger and more bearable. The dance was English, but only on the raised platform where the Lord Mayor had dined; the other tables, however, were all occupied again by men who, as usual, drank enormously the whole night. The most curious thing, though, is that a part of the company went on dancing without hearing a single note of the music, for first at one table, then at another, some were yelling songs and some swilling it down and drinking toasts amid terrific roars of 'Hurray, Hurray, Hurray' and waving of glasses. The hall and all the other rooms are illuminated with lamps which give out an unpleasant odour. It is remarkable that the Lord Mayor requires no knife at table, for a carver cuts up everything for him in advance.

(From H. C. Robbins Landon, *Haydn*)

The Prince of Wales invited Haydn to Oatlands, near Weybridge in Surrey, the country estate of his brother the Duke of York. There he met and struck up an immediate friendship with the Duchess of York,

the daughter of the King of Prussia, who received me very graciously, and said many flattering things. She is the most delightful lady in the world, is very intelligent, plays the pianoforte and sings very nicely. I had to stay there two days,

Oatlands, the estate near Weybridge in Surrey, where Haydn was entertained by the Royal Family.

because a slight indisposition prevented her attending the concert on the first day. On the second day, however, she remained continually at my side from 10 o'clock in the evening, when the music began, to 2 o'clock in the morning. Nothing but Haydn was played. I conducted the symphonies from the pianoforte, and the sweet little thing sat beside me on my left and hummed all the pieces from memory, for she had heard them so often in Berlin.

(From H. C. Robbins Landon, *Haydn*)

Haydn's happiness was blighted when he got the news, weeks after the event, that Mozart had died in Vienna on 5 December. The impact was shattering:

For some time I was beside myself about his death, and I could not believe that Providence would so soon claim the life of such an indispensable man. I only regret that before his death he could not convince the English, who walk in darkness in this respect, of his greatness — a subject about which I have been sermonising to them every single day.

(From H. C. Robbins Landon, *Haydn*)

In that letter to Michael Puchberg in Vienna, Haydn asked to be sent a catalogue of those compositions of Mozart's still unknown in England, saying he would do all he could to promote them for the benefit of Mozart's widow, Constanze. Puchberg, a banker and like Mozart a mason, had sent him about one thousand gulden in answer to the desperate begging letters, pathetic pleas for help, Mozart wrote towards the end of his life. One thousand gulden, as Robbins Landon has pointed out, was equal to Haydn's salary in 1790 – a considerable sum. Haydn was probably unaware of Puchberg's kindness to Mozart, yet there existed an even more poignant relationship between the three men; Haydn and Puchberg – 'I am inviting only Haydn and yourself' – had attended the very first piano rehearsals of Mozart's opera *Così fan tutte* scarcely two years earlier.

Haydn returned to Vienna in the summer of 1792, having extended his stay in London in order to give more concerts for Salomon. At one of these the Surprise Symphony was premièred. The composition rapidly acquired its nickname from the sudden and unexpected fortissimo chord that shatters the calm of the slow movement. The day after the concert the *Oracle* of 24 March reported:

The Second Movement was equal to the happiest of this Master's conceptions. The surprise might not be unaptly likened to the situation of a beautiful Shepherdess who, lulled to slumber by the murmur of a distant waterfall, starts alarmed by the unexpected firing of a fowling-piece.

The novelty of implanting an unexpected and violent chord within a quiet passage of music was no mere caprice, even for Haydn. On the contrary, it was a publicity stunt to steal a march on a rival composer, Ignaz Pleyel. Pleyel was Haydn's most celebrated pupil. His music was performed all over Europe – in some areas more successfully than Haydn's. Today he is regarded as little more than a shallow and inferior imitator, condemned, like so many once-popular composers, to oblivion. But, in the spring of 1792, Pleyel was the secret weapon in a war that waged between Salomon and the rival Professional Concerts organisation. Envious of Salomon's success with Haydn, the directors of the Professional Concerts series consequently brought Pleyel to London, hoping to win back their lost audience, as Griesinger relates in his biography of Haydn:

Ignaz Pleyel. (Thomas Hardy)

I asked Haydn once in jest if it were true that he wrote the kettledrum beat in order to awaken the English public that had gone to sleep at his concert. 'No', he answered me. 'Rather it was my wish to surprise the public with something new, and to make a debut in a brilliant manner so as not to be outdone by my pupil Pleyel, who at that time was engaged by an orchestra in London (in the year 1792) which had begun its concert series eight days before mine. The first Allegro of my symphony was received with countless bravos, but the enthusiasm reached its highest point in the Andante with the kettledrum beat. 'Encore! Encore!' sounded from every throat, and even Pleyel complimented me on my idea.

(From H. C. Robbins Landon, *Haydn*)

The Surprise Symphony was merely one of his many works that Londoners greeted with enthusiasm. When he left for Vienna in July 1792 there was little doubt that Haydn would soon return. His journey took him through Bonn where he met a young musician who greatly impressed him. Haydn agreed to give him tuition in composition; the young man was Ludwig van Beethoven, and he was charged ten pence per lesson. Though he was only twenty-two, Beethoven's amazing, unbridled talent was evident and Haydn offered to take him on his next trip to England in 1793. That never happened, but it is interesting to speculate how musical history – and particularly musical life in London – might have altered course had Beethoven come to London with Haydn. In November 1792 Beethoven started composition lessons with him in Vienna, and then followed him to Eisenstadt where Haydn spent the following summer working once more at the court of Esterházy. Soon Haydn was stating that Beethoven's brilliance was so remarkable that he would 'in time fill the position of one of Europe's greatest composers, and I shall be proud to be able to speak of myself as his teacher' – a generous statement, for Beethoven must at times have seemed rather bumptious to Haydn, nearly forty years his senior.

Beethoven's keyboard skill was already the talk of Vienna, and there was little doubt that his career there would be successful. And so it was not Beethoven, but Johann Elssler, Haydn's valet and music copyist, who accompanied the composer when he set off on his second journey to London in January 1794. This time Haydn took up lodgings at 1 Bury Street, St James's – conveniently close to his lady-love, the widow Schroeter. As Robbins Landon observes, Mistress Schroeter resided conveniently at 6 James Street, Buckingham Gate – a pleasant stroll via St James's Palace, The Mall and St James's Park. This second visit to London was as successful as his first. At the opening concert in Hanover Square Haydn directed his new symphony, No. 99 in E Flat, the first in which he used clarinets. It was a resounding success; by now the Professional Concerts had gone out of business, and once again he was the toast of the town. The *Morning Chronicle* was ecstatic in its praise of his new symphony: 'It is one of the grandest efforts of art that we have ever witnessed. It abounds with ideas, as new in music as they are grand and impressive; it rouses and affects every emotion of the soul. It was received with rapturous applause.'

The composition was so successful it was repeated the following week during the second concert of the series. Two weeks later, Haydn presented yet another première, Symphony No. 101, 'The Clock'. Once again this was hailed, rightly, as a masterpiece, and the audience kept applauding until the first two movements were encored. A few weeks later an even greater ovation greeted another new symphony, No. 100 in G, 'The Military', which seemed to capture the mood of a Europe boiling up for war. The *Morning Chronicle* of 9 April once again reported in raptuous terms:

Another new Symphony, by Haydn, was performed, and the middle movement was again received with absolute shouts of applause. Encore! Encore! Encore! resounded from every seat: the Ladies themselves could not forbear. It is the advancing to battle; and the march of men, the sounding of the charge, the thundering of the onset, the clash of arms, the groans of the wounded, and what may well be called the hellish roar of war, increase to a climax of horrid sublimity! which, if others can conceive, he alone can execute; at least he alone hitherto has effected these wonders.

(From H. C. Robbins Landon, *Haydn*)

Haydn was tempted to settle in London permanently, but he received news that the unmusical Prince Anton had died, and foresaw

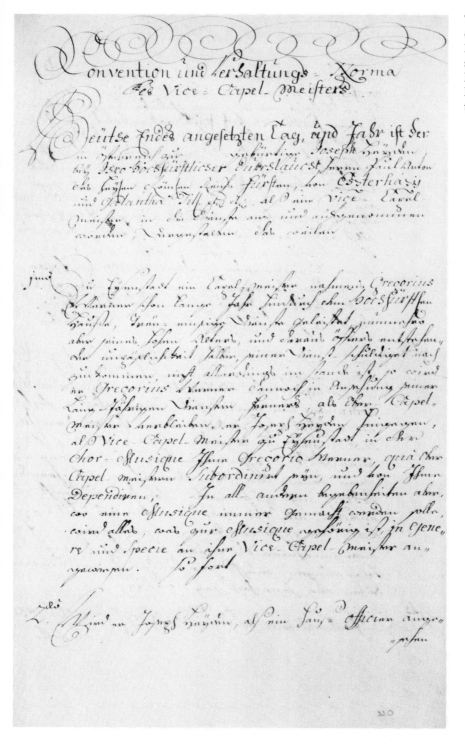

The first page of Haydn's contract of employment at Esterházy. The terms stipulated the Esterházy livery he should wear and how he should behave at all times.

that Esterházy's former glory would blossom once more under the new Prince, Nikolaus II, 'who wishes to restore the whole band again'. Nikolaus wanted Haydn to return as Kapellmeister. As his biographer, Dies, pointed out, Haydn no longer had any contractual obligations towards the Esterházys, yet his sense of loyalty remained:

> They had offered him his daily bread and (what was more important) given him the opportunity of developing his musical talents. Haydn saw, of course, that his income in England was large, and that it by far exceeded that in his fatherland. Moreover, it would have been easy for him to secure any kind of well-paid position in England. Since the death of Prince Anton, he was a completely free man; nothing bound him to the princely house except love and gratitude. It was those things, however, that silenced every opposition and persuaded him to accept the offer of Prince Nikolaus with joy and, as soon as his commitments in London were fulfilled, to return to his native country.

> (From H. C. Robbins Landon, *Haydn*)

Even so, the decision to return to his homeland across countries suffering invasion and bloodshed cannot have been easy. Haydn had grown very fond of London, and his affection for Mrs Schroeter was genuine and deeply felt. He had also become attached to the warmth of the English audiences, the sightseeing, the hospitality of the royal family, and the everyday contact with ordinary folk. In the summer of 1794 he visited Bath – 'one of the most beautiful cities in Europe' he called it – Hampton Court, Portsmouth and the Isle of Wight, and in the following February he was invited 'by the Prince of Wales to a musical soirée at the Duke of York's, which the King, the Queen, her whole family, the Duke of Orange &c. attended. Nothing else except my own compositions was played.' Other invitations followed, where he was formally introduced to other members of the royal family. King George III is reported to have spoken to Haydn in English saying, 'Doctor Haydn, you have written a great deal.' To which Haydn modestly replied, 'Yes, Sire, a great more than is good.' To which the King neatly rejoined, 'Oh no, the world contradicts that.' 'The gracious reception Haydn experienced from the King was not only gratifying to his feelings, but flattering to the science he professed.'

Haydn's supreme achievement, both in the development of the string quartet and in the symphony, was the way he made music conversational. William Mann neatly sums up Haydn's felicitous output, saying that although some of his compositions are less thrilling than others, every one of them testifies to a lively, fine, musically masterly mind completely in tune with his time. Many of them suggest that, in all history, his was the time when to be alive and a musician was, despite war, filth, penury and disease, not to mention class distinction, infinitely preferable to life at any other time. If Haydn had lived in another age, he might have written music just as idealistic, though no composer ever did.

(From W. Mann, *Music in Time*, Mitchell Beazley, 1982)

The triumphant conclusion to Haydn's years in London came with the premières of his last three symphonies, Nos. 102, 103 and 104; the last one he inscribed 'the 12th which I have composed in England'. And on 4 May a magnificent benefit concert raised the sum of 4000 gulden. Griesinger tells us that Haydn 'considered the days spent in England the happiest of his life. He was everywhere appreciated there, it opened a new world to him, and he could, through his rich earnings, at last escape the restricted circumstances in which he had grown grey.' Such comparative rewards were well earned; when Haydn catalogued the pieces he had composed either in or for England, they added up to a staggering total of more than 3000 pages of music manuscript. The symphonies he composed for Salomon account for over a third of this total.

Haydn left England on 15 August. For the rest of his life he lived mainly in Vienna, but he worked industriously, as long as his health allowed him to. These last years produced many of his finest compositions: the six great Masses, and the oratorios *The Creation* and *The Seasons*. Once again the old man proved himself to be in touch with the world around him – this time through choral music – just as his symphonies had captured the imagination of the London public. Robbins Landon points out:

Haydn had entered the hearts of his countrymen in a way that no composer had ever done to that extent previously. It is really almost as if *The Creation* was man's hope for a peaceful future (uncertain, at best, in 1799) and man's consolation for a clouded present. That it brought real comfort, consolation and joy to thousands of Viennese and, very soon, other Europeans, is clear from every document that survives. Never in the history of music, not even Handel with his *Messiah* (hardly known, for example, in France, Spain, Italy or Russia) had a composer judged the temper of his time with such smashing success.

By eighteenth-century standards, Haydn lived to an extremely old age (seventy-seven) but the habits of a lifetime stayed with him in the rigorous routine he liked to follow, as Johann Elssler described:

In the summertime he rose at half past six. The first thing he did was to shave, which he did for himself up to his 73rd year. After shaving, he got dressed completely. If a pupil were present, he had to play the lesson he had been assigned on the piano to Herr Haydn as he was dressing. The mistakes were at once corrected, the pupil instructed about the reasons thereof, and then a new task assigned. For this one and a half hours were required. On the dot of 8 o'clock breakfast had to be on the table, and right after breakfast Haydn sat down at the piano and improvised, whereby at the same time he worked out the sketch of the composition; for this, a daily period from 8 to 11·30 in the morning was required. At 11·30 visits were paid or received; or he took a walk until 1·30. From 2 to 3 o'clock was the hour for lunch. After lunch Haydn always concerned himself with some small domestic task, or he went into his small library and read a book. At 4 o'clock Haydn returned to musical affairs. He took the sketch which had been prepared that morning and put it into score, for which task he took three to four hours. At 8 pm Haydn usually went out, but came home again at 9 and either sat down to write scores or took a book and read until 10 o'clock. The hour of 10 o'clock was supper time, which consisted of bread and wine. Haydn made it a rule not to have anything else except bread and wine in the evening, and he broke the rule now and then only when he was invited out for dinner. At table Haydn liked light conversation and altogether a merry entertainment. At half past eleven Haydn went to bed — in old age even later. The wintertime made no appreciable difference in the daily schedule except that Haydn got up in the morning a half hour later, otherwise everything was as in the summer.

(From H. C. Robbins Landon, *Haydn*)

4
'There Only Remains the Task of Writing it Down'

When Joseph Haydn was on his death-bed, he could hear Napoleon's guns pounding the walls of Vienna. It was 1809 and the old Europe of Haydn and Mozart, with its patronage and its servitude, was disappearing fast. A composer who was a true product of the new age and who brought to the symphony an unprecedented power and dynamism was Ludwig van Beethoven. In the latter half of the eighteenth century the development of the string quartet and of the symphony was inextricably bound up with the idea of classical design, where detail, ornamentation, contrast and argument are controlled within a balanced and integrated shapeliness.

Ludwig van Beethoven. (Joseph Mähler)

The Greek origin of the word symphony – 'sounding together' – automatically conveys the notion of harmony, or at least of resolution – 'nature' and 'art' sharing a common bond. With hindsight we can see the matching and fulfilment of these two qualities in the symphonies Haydn and Mozart composed in their latter years. There, profound personal expression is matched by fine craftsmanship. But it was within a mere two or three generations that 'symphony' had come to mean an orchestral work of real importance. Before that it was interchangeable with 'overture'. The orchestral suites of J. S. Bach, Handel and other Baroque composers are seen as precursors of a specifically instrumental style, but it was really in the opera-houses of the courts of Europe that the pre-Classical symphony began to emerge with a distinctive structure and mood. As we have seen, it was customary to quell the disturbance of latecomers with a sinfonia before the opera proper commenced. This *sinfonia avanti l'opera* usually fell into three contrasting sections, fast – slow – fast, the standard pattern in Italian opera. The French, as always, did things their own way and preferred to start the sinfonia with a solemn, somewhat bombastic first section. The middle 'movement' was in a much livelier tempo and fugal in style. A lightweight dance section would round it all off. As time went on, these instrumental symphonies were played on other occasions, developing a life of their own, divorced from the opera-house. Disregarding all the countless manuscripts that have since disappeared, such symphonies seem to have been churned out in their thousands throughout the eighteenth century. One scholarly source lists 12,350, 'many of solid competence', as having survived from the period 1720–1820, many of them still in manuscript, in archives as far apart as Finland and Sicily, Kiev and North Carolina. These 'symphonies' are hardly of Brucknerian proportions either in duration or orchestration. Most early pre-Classical symphonies rarely extended beyond a dozen or so bars in each of their three movements.

By the 1730s, the 'standard' orchestra consisted of two oboes, two horns, a harpsichord and a small section of stringed instruments. We have seen that right up to the end of the century the presence of a keyboard player was taken for granted, even when not actually specified in the score; Haydn directed his symphonies from the piano during his visits to London. In opulent establishments this nucleus of players might be supplemented by huntsmen and military bandsmen from private militias, frequently an established part of the retinue. But it was rare that circumstances permitted anything approaching the number of players used for 'authentic' performances today. Haydn, for example, never had more than two dozen players in his orchestra at Esterházy. With himself as concertmaster, he had eleven violins, and two each of violas, cellos, double-basses, oboes, bassoons and horns. Woodwind players then, as today, were extremely versatile and could swap between flutes, oboes and even clarinets, which started to appear around the 1750s.

If *ad hoc* trumpets and drums were available, the musical role was never more than rudimentary. Indeed the kettledrum player rarely had his own part to play from, but busked it instead, joining in with the trumpeters, looking over their shoulders, making it up as he went along. No musicologist has ever satisfactorily explained why the style of trumpet-writing dropped off so abruptly from the florid and immensely difficult writing that we find in Bach's music to the lumpen bugle-notes found in the pre-Classical symphony. It seems to have happened within a single generation, and was not merely the result of changing tastes and musical fashions. It has been suggested that the old guilds of town trumpeters closed ranks to safeguard the secrets of their craft – an early example of the closed shop! Inevitably, their skills would have died with them. Very quickly, the elaborate, often stratospheric, trumpet parts of Bach's style were regarded as old-fashioned as composers of the Rococo explored different paths.

Oddly, the tradition of horn playing did not suffer in the same way, kept alive no doubt by the aristocracy's insatiable love of hunting, and the skilled bands of horn players employed on estates – especially in Bohemia. On occasions, Haydn's symphonies include horn passages of great daring. When he composed, it is clear that he had specific players in mind, giving the double-basses a moment of glory, or devoting an entire *legato* movement to an oboist.

As we have seen at Mannheim, the symphonic repertoire expanded beyond all recognition. At its zenith, Mannheim boasted an orchestra of huge proportions by eighteenth-century standards: a thirty-four-piece string section, two flutes, two oboes and two clarinets (whose sound filled Mozart with ecstasy) and four bassoons, two horns and kettledrums. Such was the strength of the Elector's private militia that Stamitz and his colleagues could summon as many as a dozen trumpeters when occasion demanded.

When the Palatine court moved to Munich, and the glory that was Mannheim faded, many of those Mannheim musicians moved on to Vienna. As the century progressed Vienna assumed growing importance as a musical centre, the inevitable result of the city's geographical position as the 'crossroads of European civilisation'. It became the focal point of political and cultural interests from all parts of the sprawling mass of the Austro-Hungarian Empire. It attracted wealth in the form of politicians and statesmen, entrepreneurs and administrators, courtiers, diplomats, businessmen and hangers-on. As far as musicians were concerned, each was a potential patron, and it is little wonder that the city was to become a creative powerhouse, attracting the best talents, just as Mannheim had done. With such an abundance of wealth, Vienna acted as a magnet for a host of minor composers in the middle of the eighteenth century, long before the city became linked with such composers as Mozart, Haydn, Beethoven and Schubert.

In Vienna, and in Mannheim, music was composed as on a production line. In Vienna, for example, Carl Ditters von Dittersdorf (by no means an insignificant figure in the development of the symphony) composed at least 130 'symphonies'. In the second half of the eighteenth century, London also had its fair share of glory; symphonies, as we have seen, formed a prominent part of the public concerts given regularly by the 'London' Bach, Johann Christian, and his compatriot Carl Friedrich Abel. Both were skilful and tuneful composers who dominated London's musical life, inheriting at least some of the limelight after Handel's death in 1759, the year Abel arrived in London. Like so many Germans of the period, the musical outlook of Abel and J. C. Bach was thoroughly Italianate; their melodic gift was breezy, operatic and lyrical, their sense of structure well-punctuated and clearly defined.

As an eight-year-old child in London, Mozart had copied out in his own handwriting a symphony by Abel. For a long time musicologists took that manuscript to be an original Mozart composition. But Wolfgang had copied it merely as a way to study a composition, not with the intention to deceive; it was a chore customarily expected of any apprentice composer. But in spring 1765 he did compose in London his Symphony in D Major which demonstrated a degree of maturity remarkable in a child of eight or nine. Later on, as he gained familiarity with the Viennese tradition – both the older school of composers and the recently produced symphonies of Haydn – his skills were further enriched.

By the time Haydn took up his position at the court of Esterházy in 1761, many of the characteristics of the Classical symphony were clearly defined, if not totally established. Haydn was nearly thirty before he had any incentive to compose symphonies. The stability of a permanent orchestra and the pressure of writing to a regular deadline enabled him to experiment and acquire skill in handling symphonic materials. By dint of hard work, therefore, he had produced many works of great power and originality by the time Mozart visited Vienna in the summer of 1773.

Mozart's understanding of the orchestra was also enriched by his experience of music in Paris. One of his constant complaints was that the standard of instrument-playing in Salzburg was very low. In Paris, however, he relished the opportunity to write for an orchestra considerably larger than was available to him in Salzburg. Typically, his imagination responded fully to the wider range of tone-colours – just as it always responded to meeting a pressing deadline. But the Viennese, who should have opened their purses to 'the composer of *Figaro*', did not load him with lucrative commissions.

Only a few years later they were faced with another rising star – Beethoven – and when he set out from Bonn on the journey to Vienna, the musical capital of Europe, everyone's good wishes went with him, as a note from Count Waldstein of November 1792 indicates:

Dear Beethoven,
You are going to Vienna in fulfilment of your long-frustrated wishes. The Genius of Mozart is still mourning and weeping over the death of her pupil. She found a refuge but no occupation with the inexhaustible Haydn; through him she wishes

have decided that Fate at the door is more appropriate than a little songbird. It is more compellingly theatrical and it fits in much better with the jutting jaw, the furrowed brow, the idealist, the 'democrat incarnate', as Emerson called him.

But Beethoven's music grew out of the eighteenth century, just as truly as it heralded the new aspirations of Europe after the French Revolution. After all, he used the same raw materials as Haydn, Mozart or any of his immediate predecessors. The difference was in how he manipulated those raw materials. In his Fifth Symphony there are several instances where Beethoven's melodies echo Mozart's. Themes from the finale of Mozart's Symphony No. 40 in G Minor and from the slow movement of No. 41 in C turn up in a different guise in the last two movements of Beethoven's Fifth. This is hardly coincidence; if you look in the particular manuscript sketchbook where Beethoven roughed out his ideas for this symphony, you find he copied out two and a half dozen bars of the finale of Mozart's Fortieth Symphony. However, mere thematic similarities between the work of one composer and another tell us little except that both composers share a common vocabulary. Originality and enterprise lie not in the notes but in the way they are used, and in his Third Symphony, the 'Eroica', Beethoven established a completely new category of utterance, purposely and irrevocably redefining the symphony as a medium of expression. For one thing the duration of the 'Eroica' – fifty minutes – is twice that of most symphonies by Haydn and Mozart. Its clashing dissonances and the raging, uncompromising dynamism of its accents were totally without precedent.

The central symbol of Beethoven's divorce from the old world was its dedicatee, Napoleon, the outward embodiment of a revolution that had burst out of France and threatened to engulf the whole of Europe. For many Romantic artists, the Revolution offered freedom of thought as well as political freedom – the dawn of a new age where men were to be valued for their worth and not for their birth. The slogan of 'Liberty, Equality and Brotherhood' was shouted around Europe with little thought for the brutality and the hardship that the Revolution, and Napoleon's conquering army, had inflicted, not only on the moneyed ruling classes, but also on the common man, he whom it was thought necessary to liberate. The symbol of Napoleon-the-Invincible concealed the horror and the bloodshed.

However compelling these external circumstances, Beethoven, before the age of thirty, had to face up to his own intensely personal tragedy. On one level he had everything to look forward to. He had stunned Viennese society with the brilliance of his piano playing and his phenomenal ability to improvise at the keyboard. Financially, he could rely on several important and wealthy aristocrats who were prepared to pay handsomely to be the dedicatees of any new composition. Yet, behind all this, and however much he tried to conceal the fact, his world was crumbling around him. The terrible fear that had haunted him for some years was now reality; his growing deafness was incurable. His doctors suggested he spend the summer away from Vienna, in the village of Heiligenstadt. There, he might have a chance to recuperate in the peace of the countryside. But he remained deeply

The last page of Beethoven's will, written in 1802 when he realised that his deafness was incurable.

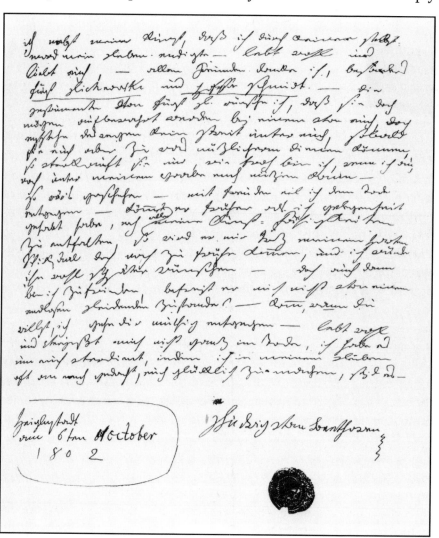

depressed and in October 1802, shortly before his thirty-second birthday, he sat down to write his will:

Oh, you, my fellow men who think, or say, that I am morose, stubborn or misanthropic, how greatly do you wrong me. From childhood my heart and spirit were full of tenderness and goodwill, and I was always conscious of achieving great things even. But understand that for six years my condition has been incurable, aggravated by senseless physicians, deceived year after year in hoping I'd recover, finally compelled to face up to a permanent affliction, which may last for years or be impossible to cure. But how could I possibly say to people: 'Speak up, because I'm deaf'. How could I, of all people, conceivably admit an infirmity in the one sense that should have been more perfect in me than in others? So you must forgive me if I shrink away when I'd much rather stay amongst you, and it's doubly painful to be so misunderstood. I have to live like an exile, for when I'm with people I'm terrified they might discover what is wrong with me. How humiliating when somebody standing right next to me could hear a flute in the distance, and I heard nothing, or when they could hear the song of a shepherd boy and I couldn't hear a thing. Such incidents brought me to the verge of despair; anything more and I'd have killed myself. One thing only – my art – held me back. I could not leave the world until I had produced all I felt called upon to produce.

(From H. C. Robbins Landon, *Beethoven*)

That he had contemplated suicide indicates how bitterly cheated Beethoven must have felt; a young and brilliantly talented composer in his early thirties, baring his soul in terms of such bleak despair. It is tempting to search in the music he was writing that summer to find this grief encapsulated in his compositions. However, we know for certain that at the time he was completing his Second Symphony, a work that could never be described as glum or defeatist. On the contrary, apart from its solemn opening pages, it is characterised by bountiful vitality and fun. This is another instance when it is nonsense to interpret a composer's work in terms of his day-to-day circumstances. Likewise, the few facts we know about the origin of Beethoven's Third Symphony have been completely swept aside in a flood of historical conjecture. Beethoven's pupil Ferdinand Ries (who recounted how he had stood next to him on the occasion when the shepherd boy's flute was inaudible to the composer) tells us something of the background:

In this symphony, Beethoven had Bonaparte in mind – but as he was when he was First Consul. Beethoven esteemed him greatly at the time and likened him to the greatest Roman consuls. I, as well as several of Beethoven's more intimate friends, saw a copy of the score lying upon his table, with the word 'Bonaparte' at the extreme top of the title page, and at the extreme bottom 'Luigi van Beethoven' – but not another word. Whether and with what the space between was to be

The title-page of the manuscript of the 'Eroica' Symphony.

filled out, I do not know. I was the first to bring him the news that Bonaparte had proclaimed himself Emperor, whereupon he flew into a rage and cried out: 'Is he then, too, nothing more than an ordinary human being? Now he, too, will trample on the rights of man and indulge only his ambition. He will exalt himself above all others, become a tyrant!' Beethoven went to the table, took hold of the title page by the top, tore it in two, and threw it on the floor. The first page was rewritten and only then did the symphony receive the title *Sinfonia Eroica*.

(From H. C. Robbins Landon, *Beethoven*)

In fact the nickname 'Eroica' did not attach itself to the symphony until two years later. However disgusted Beethoven might have been at the time, he subsequently referred to 'a new grand symphony' in a letter to the publishers Breitkopf and Härtel, dated 26 August 1804. In it he specifically adds 'the title of the symphony is really Bonaparte', and never felt obliged to cross out the words he had written in pencil on his own copy of the score – '*Geschrieben auf Bonaparte*' ('written on Bonaparte'). The question persists, if Beethoven had set out to celebrate a specific hero – Napoleon – why did the inscription remain after that hero had become *persona non grata*?

There are more ambiguities. How do we account for the last movement of the symphony, lifted directly from a ballet score, *Prometheus*, he had written a couple of years previously? Prometheus was a demigod, son of a Titan. He created man out of clay and stole fire from the gods on Mount Olympus. Here is the same Prometheus music providing an inexorable conclusion to the 'Eroica' Symphony. Further, how do we interpret the symphony's subtitle, *'composta per festiggiare il sovvenire d'un grand'Uomo'* ('composed to celebrate the memory of a great man')? Are we to take it that Beethoven, thoroughly disillusioned, now thought of Napoleon as a *once* great man?

Opinions vary as to the identity of the real hero. Was it Beethoven himself? Was it Nelson? Was it General Abercromby, who also died in the Napoleonic Wars, at the Battle of Alexandria in 1801? Or was it the Unknown Soldier, representing all the Austrian dead? Was it a generalised concept of heroism *per se*? There has never been a shortage of candidates for the vacancy. It has even been suggested that Beethoven (having composed at the age of twenty a very fine cantata honouring the memory of his dead monarch Joseph II of Austria) waited patiently for ten years and then turned quisling. While Napoleon's armies were defeating Austria in 1800 in a blood-bath of horrendous ferocity, Beethoven, it has been alleged, planned to slip across the border into France, retaining the 'Buonaparte' ascriptions, written on the score in Italian, to save his own skin! Such wild conjecture makes little sense, but then virtually every note Beethoven composed has been interpreted in terms of the French Revolution at some time or another.

In his first two symphonies Beethoven had continued broadly on the lines of Haydn and Mozart and in his Third he certainly burst out of the eighteenth century like La Grande Armée had out of France. In every aspect of technique – in thematic shaping, in harmony, in the violence of its cross-rhythms, in its proportions, and in the idea of symphonic form – it defied established order. In the old world, Mozart, Haydn and others had carried on in the belief that what was there today would still be there tomorrow. In their ideas of musical form, things ended much as they began. The essence of the Classical first movement, for example, was symmetrical: A – B – A. That is to say a group of themes would be presented, explored in a central 'development section', and then recapitulated in the light of experience. That sort of symmetry was impossible for Beethoven: he had little compulsion to pursue a musical tour twice round the same country.

How did Beethoven set to work? We have a good idea, for he worked in sketchbooks, of which about fifty survive. They are

Prince Carl Lichnowsky, skilled musician, connoisseur of the arts and devoted friend of Beethoven and Mozart, with whom he had studied. The Prince was one of Beethoven's staunchest supporters and for a time they lived in the same house and shared the same servant.

detailed accounts of his work extending over most of his career, one project overlapping another, musical ideas jotted down one day, reaching fruition in years to come. Quite apart from his grapplings with the compositions that we know about, it has been estimated that there are sketches for some eighty other pieces.

Once a theme has occurred to me [he said] I can remember it for years. I alter it considerably, rejecting and experimenting until I am satisfied. The development begins in my head, whether in concentrating on the idea, the breadth of treatment, or the pitch – high or low. Since I know what I want, the basic idea never deserts me. It rises and grows. I hear and see the complete picture . . . there only remains the task of writing it down.

(From H. C. Robbins Landon, *Beethoven*)

The sketchbooks, with their innumerable crossings-out, revisions and second thoughts, suggest that this latter process was not as straightforward as Beethoven suggested:

Where the ideas come from, I do not know. I do not seek them, directly or indirectly. I could grasp them in my hands, walking out of doors in the woods, in the middle of the night or in the early morning. A poet translates such moods into words: I turn them into sounds.

(From H. C. Robbins Landon, *Beethoven*)

A typical page of one of Beethoven's sketchbooks. This passage eventually became part of the Pastoral Symphony.

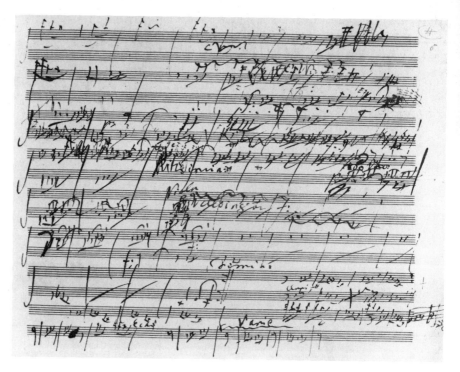

The courtly pomp of
Versailles provided one of the
first 'modern' orchestras: this
painting shows the
magnificent château and
gardens. (Patel the Elder)

Louis XIV at the establishment of the Academy of Science and the founding of the Observatory in 1667 (Testelin). He was known for his interest in all types of culture.

After 1720 Mannheim (opposite, above) became the administrative capital of the Elector Palatine. Its spacious vistas, gardens and buildings rivalled Versailles.

Early in the eighteenth century a distinctive 'violinistic' style of composition had developed, based on established melodic and harmonic patterns. The most brilliant exponent of this was Antonio Vivaldi, who composed innumerable works for the young ladies of the Ospedale Santa Maria in Venice (opposite, below), an orphanage where he was director of music. (Guardi)

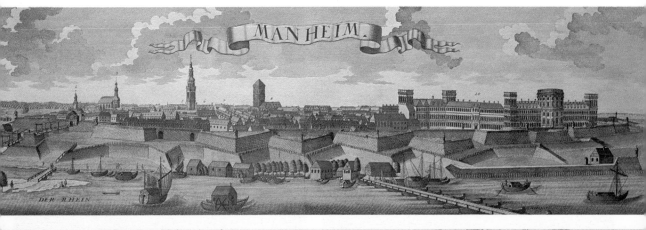

Above, left: Leopold Mozart
(attrib. Della Croce)

Above, right: Wolfgang aged
six (Lorenzoni). He was given
this suit by the Empress
Maria Theresa to wear in
1762. It is said to have been
made for the young
Archduke Maximilian, born
in the same year as Wolfgang.

Right: Maria Anna (Nannerl)
Mozart (attrib. Lorenzoni)

Opposite: The Empress Maria
Theresa and family. (Martin
van Meytens)

The Nymphenburg Palace
outside Munich, where
Wolfgang made his first
major appearance. (Bellotto)

The Mozarts did a great deal of sightseeing in London. Nannerl's diary recounted their visit to St Paul's; the opulent Venetian barges are no doubt a fanciful exaggeration by the artist, Canaletto.

Mozart at the harpsichord
with Nannerl and Leopold
(Louis de Carmontelle).
Copies of this picture were
distributed by Leopold as
publicity handouts.

Opposite : Venice's wealth
had cultivated an
extraordinary range of
instrumental and vocal
music-making. The Mozarts
visited the city in 1771
during carnival season.
Carpaccio's painting captures
the colour and festivity of
this time of year.

Mozart playing the
harpsichord at the Conti
Court. (Michel Barthélemy
Olliver)

'Musician at the harpsichord' by Duplessis. This is thought to be Mozart as a young man.

Left: An unfinished portrait
of Mozart by the Viennese
actor and painter Joseph
Lange, the husband of
Aloysia Weber, Mozart's
sister-in-law and first love.

Opposite: The Rittersaal in
the Palace of the Elector
Palatine where many new
works by Mannheim
composers were premièred.
Mozart played here before
the Elector Karl Theodor.

Above: The palace of the
Esterházy family at Mariahilf
in Vienna in 1800.
Right: The magnificent gates
of the Esterházy summer
palace at Fertod in Hungary.

A reconstruction of the music room at Eisenstadt, where Haydn would present new compositions to Prince Nikolaus and his guests.

Hanover Square, one of the centres of London musical life at the end of the eighteenth century. The famous concert-hall where Haydn appeared was in Hanover Street (left background).

Johann Peter Salomon in 1791, the year he introduced Haydn to English audiences. (Thomas Hardy)

Joseph Haydn in 1791. (Thomas Hardy)

Left: Beethoven as a young man (Christian Horneman). He astonished the Viennese with his tempestuous piano-playing and Mozart, having heard him improvise at a Viennese soirée, said: 'Mark my words, that young chap will cause quite a stir in the world.'

Below: David's painting of the ceremony in 1804 in Notre Dame when Napoleon Bonaparte took the crown from Pope Pius VII and crowned himself Emperor.

'Liszt at the piano' by
Danhauser. Liszt is
surrounded by (left to right)
Alexandre Dumas, Berlioz,
George Sand, Paganini,
Rossini and Liszt's mistress,
the Countess Marie d'Agoult.

Hector Berlioz. (Signol, detail)

Maria Malibran in the role of Desdemona in Rossini's *Otello* (Decaisne, detail). This tempestuous Spanish mezzo-soprano made her operatic debut when she was seventeen; but her brilliant international career was brought to a tragic end at the age of twenty-eight when she was fatally injured in a riding accident.

Arnold Schoenberg, whose music transformed the traditions of tonality and introduced new concepts of symphony. (Richard Gerstl)

Normally he would work on several compositions at once. He started the Fifth Symphony before the Fourth, which interrupted it in mid-flow. At the same time he wrote the Sixth, the 'Pastoral'. Indeed, the Fifth and the Sixth were originally numbered in reverse order when premièred in the same concert. Moreover, Beethoven was composing not just symphonies but also other categories of music, in abundance. In 1805, for example, when what we call the Fifth Symphony was

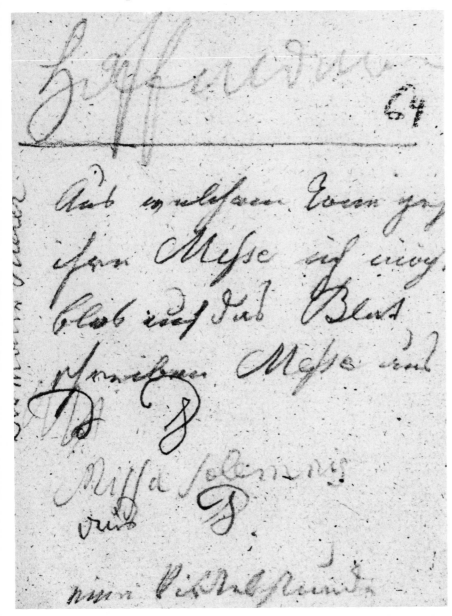

A page from one of Beethoven's conversation books, dated April 1820.

begun, he was also composing Piano Concerto No. 4; these are two very different works (although it has been suggested that the rhythm that opens Beethoven's Fifth happens also to be the nuclear start of Piano Concerto No. 4 in a muted form).

Music was in Beethoven's head all the time as it was in Mozart's, making opus numbers irrelevant. If no single composition chronologically followed any other, then in some God-given mystery, the music was forever there, past, present and future, and all they had to do – Beethoven, Schubert and Mozart especially – was to collate it all in terms of dots and dashes on parallel lines, to organise the print-out, so to speak, that lesser mortals might reproduce it as best they can.

How are those dots and dashes written down, and how accurate are they? Musical notation can be hopelessly vague at times, even when dealing with fundamental ingredients; loud and soft, long and short. Let us forget about Fate knocking on the door and yellow-hammers in the Praterpark and instead examine the pause that is marked over the fourth note – the long one – that opens Beethoven's Fifth. It is also marked *ff* – fortissimo (very loud). The question is how long is the pause to be held? How loud is loud? And when a composer like Stravinsky specifies 'loud' is it the same degree of loudness, or the same quality of attack, as when you play 'loud' in Mozart?

It is clearly not so, and the job of an orchestral conductor or an interpretive musician is never an exact science. For this reason no artist or record reviewer can claim that a certain interpretation is definitive. No two instrumentalists, no two conductors, and no two performances can ever be identical. And the greater the composition, the more a musician's understanding of it is likely to change and mature over the years, since every time he performs it he discovers new details in the piece – and in himself. The question inevitably arises: How could Beethoven, when deafness overtook him, really know what he was writing? It is not a foolish question, because composers frequently rephrase, reorchestrate, or even restructure entire sections of a new composition after hearing it performed.

Beethoven was denied that luxury, but he was not prevented from carrying in his head his final concept of how those elements were to fit together. Just as a non-composer can put words on paper – and can understand those words without having to hear them out loud – so a composer learns to put musical notes onto manuscript paper. Beethoven knew precisely what he was doing and understood the tone-colours of the instruments he used, the physical tension of high notes, the rhythmic and harmonic effects he was creating. As far as we can tell his hearing problems did not start until he was in his late twenties and many years were to elapse before he went totally deaf. His hearing would come and go, variable and unpredictable, which must have been intensely frustrating. At times it would be nearly normal and he was still performing in public, as a pianist, when he was in his mid-thirties, though often with enormous difficulty and lamentable results:

It was not a treat, for, in the first place, the pianoforte was badly out of tune, which Beethoven minded little since he did not hear it; secondly, there was scarcely

Louis Spohr (self-portrait), German composer, violinist and conductor, whose orchestral music has, unjustifiably, dropped out of fashion.

anything left of the virtuosity of the artist which had formerly been so greatly admired. In *forte* passages the poor deaf man pounded on the keys till the strings jangled, and in *piano* he played so softly that whole groups of notes were omitted, so that the music was unintelligible unless one could look into the pianoforte part.

(From A. W. Thayer, *Life of Beethoven*, Vol. II, Centaur Press, 1960)

This report by a fine musician, German composer, conductor and violinist Louis Spohr, describes a rehearsal in 1814 when Beethoven played the piano part in his Piano Trio in B Flat (The Archduke). It must have been torture for his fellow players, not merely because of the incompetence of Beethoven's playing, but because of the need to hide their concern from him. Spohr adds: 'I was deeply saddened at so hard a fate; Beethoven's continual melancholy was no longer a riddle to me.' To Beethoven, deafness was not so much a technical handicap but a social, day-to-day frustration. As he became increasingly cut off from the world, so he withdrew into his own private world of imagination, as his last string quartets and piano sonatas testify. So, in that sense, his deafness certainly affected what he wrote.

We tend to think of Beethoven solely as a composer, but he was a very practical musician, a gifted pianist with a brilliant technique, once lionised in the salons of Viennese aristocracy. The première of a new Beethoven composition was a great social event as well as being a musical landmark. So it was deeply humiliating for him, and appallingly embarrassing, when deafness overtook him and he could hear only the loud sections of the music. He completed his Seventh Symphony, for example, in May 1812, when he was forty-one and at the height of his fame. For months he seems to have postponed the première, perhaps saving this new major work for a visit to London, which had been proposed (but which never took place). Beethoven himself conducted the première in Vienna and Spohr gives us a vivid account of the way Beethoven directed the orchestra – an orchestra which included many distinguished musicians as well as Spohr.

Although much had been told me about his way of conducting, it nevertheless astounded me to the utmost degree. He was in the habit of giving dynamic indications to the orchestra by means of all sorts of peculiar movements of his body. When he wanted a *sforzando*, he would vehemently throw out both his arms, which previously he had held across his breast. For a *piano* he would crouch down, going deeper and deeper as he wanted the sound to be softer.

Then at the beginning of a *crescendo* he would rise gradually and when the *forte* was reached he would leap into the air. The execution was quite masterly despite Beethoven's uncertain and sometimes ludicrous conducting. It was evident that the poor deaf master was no longer able to hear the *pianos* in his music. This was particu-

larly evident in a passage where two pauses are marked over two consecutive chords
– the first one loud, the second soft. Beethoven had probably overlooked the second
one, because he started off beating time again before the orchestra had even reached
the second pause. Therefore, without realising it, he was ahead of the orchestra
by as much as ten or twelve bars when it began to play the *pianissimo*.

Indicating the passage in his own way, Beethoven had crouched down under
the music stand; at the *crescendo* which followed he became visible once more, making himself taller, and then leapt high in the air at the moment when he *thought*
the *forte* should have begun. When it did not materialise, he looked about in terror,
stared astonished at the orchestra (which was still playing *pianissimo*) and found
his place only when the so-long-awaited *forte* began and became audible to him.

(From A. W. Thayer, Life of Beethoven, Vol. II)

The story is unbelievably sad, but it does tell us quite a lot about
Beethoven's interpretation of his own music, particularly the dramatic
and wildly contrasting dynamics, the exaggeration between extremes
of loudness and softness. Eventually, there would usually be a skilled
musician standing at Beethoven's elbow, ready to give that vital nod
or a tactful upbeat when the performance seemed likely to fall apart.

By all accounts the players themselves respected him, this stocky,
floundering windmill of a man. Indeed, that first performance of the
Seventh Symphony was such a success that the audience demanded
an encore of the slow movement. The critics, however, were not quite

Carl Maria Weber conducting
Der Freischütz at Covent
Garden. He was one of the
first to use a baton – grasped
in the middle and extremely
heavy.

so impressed. The finale of this symphony was singled out as 'absurd, untamed music'. Beethoven was deemed to have created 'the acme of shapelessness', 'a delirium, in which there is no trace of melody or harmony, no single sound to fall gratefully upon the ear'. Weber – the composer of *Der Freischütz*, and sixteen years Beethoven's junior – later heard the piece performed in Leipzig and said, 'On the strength of the Seventh Symphony, Beethoven should be locked away in a madhouse.' Others simply said that when Beethoven composed the first and fourth movements, he must have been drunk.

In concert-halls today this work is the most frequently performed of all Beethoven's symphonies, and it is difficult now to comprehend why it should have provoked such hostility. He himself looked upon this symphony with great fondness, regarding it as one of his best works. Melodically it is glorious; rhythmically it has immense verve; and its overall sense of design is perfect. Richard Wagner – who could never resist the temptation of imposing a story-line on any piece of music, however abstract – described Beethoven's Seventh as 'the apotheosis of the dance'. He apparently pranced around the room improvising a balletic interpretation of the symphony while Franz Liszt thrashed it out on the piano. (What one would give to have been there!)

The original objections to the symphony seemed to start with the opening pages, where Beethoven rapidly shifts the harmonic 'centre of gravity' from A major to C major. To us, those chords do not conflict with each other, but to Beethoven's contemporaries they were unpleasantly dissonant. The fact is that we are so used to noise, to transistor radios, rock-and-roll and all that has been composed in the years since Beethoven, that our ears have lost their innocence.

Critics also found fault with the way Beethoven at times seemed simply to be fooling around aimlessly, as he leads into a livelier tempo in the first movement – a transition that to us seems playfully innocent. He also writes passages that seem simply to run up and down the scale. At another point the music develops 'hiccups'. Half the problem was that nobody could ever bring themselves to admit that the great Beethoven possessed a sense of humour. Of course, although he repeatedly took liberties in this symphony, using musical ideas that in themselves seem trite, beneath this jokiness there was an assured hand at work. The theme of the second movement, for example, played by itself as a melodic line means nothing. The tune repeats the same note a dozen times, before it staggers with considerable

The procession at Beethoven's funeral.

banality to adjacent notes. Yet that apparently undistinguished theme first appeared in one of his sketchbooks six years previously, suggesting that those sketchbooks were largely an *aide-mémoire*. The theme is worthless unless one assumes that for six years Beethoven carried in his mind its full potential : harmony, counter-melodies, its cumulative power and the darkness of its initial orchestration. Otherwise the line of notes, as scribbled in the sketchbook, makes no sense at all. When Beethoven builds up from that seemingly idiotic tune, you soon realise that just around the corner a vast and processional climax is lurking. He compounds the mystery by starting the movement – as he concludes it – with an extraordinary chord, curiously voiced, with no bass note to root it in reality.

He reshaped and reworked trite ideas, yet the final version seems utterly spontaneous as in the Seventh Symphony; the mark of the true artist – *ars est celare artem* – is to conceal the artistry he puts into his work; the ability to take the basic raw materials – the bricks and mortar – and to build from them something fresh and supremely imaginative.

5
'Spirit of Romance'

The Danhauser portrait of Liszt and friends painted in 1840 (see page 98) looks very much like a pictorial 'Who's Who in Romanticism'. In addition to Liszt, the most flamboyant pianist the world has ever seen, we see Marie d'Agoult, his mistress, at his feet; sitting in the chair is Chopin's mistress, George Sand, in male attire and a red cloak; next to her is the novelist Alexandre Dumas; behind him is Hector Berlioz, standing next to Paganini and Rossini. Overlooking them all, dominating the assembly with a heavy symbolism, is the bust of Beethoven, larger than life. (Some sources identify the person standing behind Dumas as Victor Hugo, but others as Berlioz.)

It is extraordinary to think of so many different talents appearing at the same time. Berlioz and Glinka, powerful creative innovators in their respective environments, France and Russia, were born in 1803, when Beethoven was working on his epic 'Eroica' Symphony. At the end of that decade Liszt, Chopin, Mendelssohn and Schumann were born, the four of them within eighteen months of each other; Verdi and Wagner, the two giants of nineteenth-century opera, and direct contemporaries, were both born a few years later in 1813. By 1830, when Beethoven and Schubert were dead, these young lions were ready to roar, and roar they did. And none so loud as the wild-headed Frenchman, Hector Berlioz. Beethoven had established the right of every creative artist to assert his artistic personality; the absolute right of expression on nobody's terms but his own. The composer, in a word, was his own man and the audience had to tag along as best it could. What was the Romantic composer to express? How was this self-expression to be achieved?

The answer was for the composer to use himself as a sounding-board. What was important was his response to and perception of external stimuli: the agony of love, a gothic fantasy, the adoration of the countryside in all its moods, the terror of the supernatural, a fairy-tale land of make-believe, translated into evocative orchestral colours, expressive harmonies and soul-searching melody. Best of all, the Romantic composer could set himself up as his own hero. If he were ever short of subject matter he could always express the unbear-

Caricature of Hector Berlioz. One of the few composers of the Romantic period who was not a good pianist, he thought instinctively in orchestral terms.

able anguish of simply being a Romantic, a solitary figure battling against odds in a hostile world.

But any piece of music requires a formal shape, some architectural design, otherwise it is nothing more than aimless rambling. In the musical styles of the eighteenth century the problem hardly arose; composers tended to think intuitively in patterns that were formally balanced, logical, controlled. One aspect of Romanticism was to throw off the constraints of Classical design, to reject the shackles and to be free. How else is the Romantic spirit to express its own identity? You cannot construct a gothic castle if you shape it like the Parthenon.

This problem of construction never troubled some composers. Mendelssohn, for example, thought quite naturally in terms of Classical and balanced design; the proportions and shapeliness of his music demonstrate, in every bar, that large-scale forms like the symphony held no terrors for him. But for many other composers, shorter forms were the solution — the cameo, the treasured moment, the fleeting scene beautifully captured in a short piano piece, or an emotional outpouring in a 'song without words' or, better still, song *with* words. In this way a composer need never face up to the problem of structuring a long piece of music. Shorter pieces are much easier to construct; by the time the material has exhausted itself, it is time to stop anyway. But the imagination of Hector Berlioz extended to infinitely wider horizons, challenging conventional attitudes towards structure and orchestral colour.

Even as a medical student Berlioz knew without doubt that his soaring imagination could be expressed only in a musical career:

Become a doctor! Study anatomy! Dissect! Take part in horrible operations — instead of giving myself body and soul to music — sublime art whose grandeur I was beginning to perceive? Forsake the highest heaven for the wretchedest regions of earth, the immortal spirits of poetry and love? No! No!

His father, a well-to-do doctor, had always objected to his son's wish to become a composer. To please his parents, Berlioz had studied medicine for a time. Before long he threw all his energies into music, determined to make a name for himself. Eventually he succeeded though financial rewards were few. As a student, he won the coveted prize of the French Conservatoire, the Prix de Rome, which at least pleased his father. But Berlioz's struggles were largely a catalogue of frustration; his extraordinary originality and artistic zeal were bound to conflict with a public attuned to the less taxing fare of Italianate opera, firmly entrenched in Paris at the time.

In Paris on 11 September 1827 Berlioz saw a play by Shakespeare for the first time. It was performed by a visiting troupe of actors from England. The company's leading lady was an Irish girl called Harriet Smithson. Berlioz fell in love with her, madly and ridiculously. The intensity of that infatuation and the twists and turns of their relationship became inextricably entangled with a symphony he was about to compose – 'Episode in the Life of an Artist' he called it. That composition turned out to be one of the most extraordinary and original works ever written – the Fantastic Symphony.

Harriet Smithson, whose portrayal of Shakespeare's tragic heroines established her as one of the most distinguished actresses of her time.

Many poets, painters and composers of the Romantic period explored a strange territory – the world of dreams – a world of self-delusion, where reality and fantasy were indistinguishable. But few creative artists lived out their lives in their work with such compulsion as Berlioz. He was obsessed by the vision of his beloved Harriet, captured in a musical theme – an *idée fixe* – an obsessive, haunting melody that stayed with him constantly, like the memory of her face. The musical theme – lonely, wistful, almost operatic in style, like an aria – recurs throughout all five movements of the symphony. Time and again the 'impressionable young composer' hears the melody in different contexts, transformed or disguised, and he catches a glimpse of his beloved wherever he turns. It haunts him in his dreams (Berlioz had come across a French translation of De Quincey's *Confessions of an Opium Eater*) and at a grand ball, and in the countryside. There is a twist to the story; suddenly our poor composer is marched off to be executed for killing his beloved, who has turned out to be a witch.

It is an odd scenario to associate with a French composer and an Irish actress, but from the moment he set eyes on her, Berlioz was utterly infatuated by Harriet – although she did nothing to encourage his affections. Indeed, for several years they never met; she avoided him and refused to open his letters.

Despite this, Berlioz continued to idolise her. To him, she was the personification of Ophelia and Juliet. To her, however, Berlioz was simply another 'stage-door Johnny'. She had been told he was mad and she pointed him out to other members of the cast, warning them 'to beware of the gentleman with eyes that bode no good'. He worshipped her from afar, prowling the streets at night, lurking in doorways, desperate to catch a glimpse of her on her way to the theatre – she, the great actress, he, the struggling composer. 'Oh, vain, ill-fated one,' he wrote. 'If you could comprehend for a moment all the poetry, all the immensity of my love. Yet, we *will* be united in the oblivion of the grave . . . Oh, how I once loved you . . . Oh, Juliet . . . Ophelia . . .'

His love rejected, only bitterness remained when Harriet left Paris and the theatre company moved on. Berlioz was distraught. How could she be so cruel as to ignore him so utterly? By this time the whole of Paris knew about Berlioz's mania. No infatuation could ever have been so public. He told his friends he wanted to set to work on a major composition, giving vent to his complex feelings towards

Marie Pleyel (Camille) and her husband Joseph Pleyel. They separated after four years and she continued her career as an international pianist.

Harriet. But he had reached a kind of mental block. 'I have it all in my head,' so he claimed, 'but I can write nothing.'

Happily a solution was just around the corner in the shapely form of a young woman called Camille. Staggeringly beautiful, Camille was also a professional musician, a brilliant pianist. Many said that her playing was as good as the young Franz Liszt, praise indeed. Camille was captivated by Berlioz, this wild young genius with his handsome good looks. For his part, Berlioz found her to be intelligent, vivacious and – unlike Harriet – accessible. The notes simply flew onto the manuscript paper. Inevitably, to justify his new amour Berlioz started to blacken Harriet's name. To kill off the memory of this 'witch', he slandered her reputation, viciously magnifying her faults, both real and imaginary. With Harriet out of the way, he now planned to marry the adorable Camille.

Harriet returned to Paris in March 1830 for another acting engagement – but with little success this time – to find the city boiling up for an outbreak of revolution. (It erupted in July.) Berlioz lay low, completing his Fantastic Symphony 'to the sound of stray bullets coming over the roofs and pattering on the wall'. Meanwhile he also put the finishing touches to his entry for the composition prize, the Prix de Rome, his fourth, and this time successful, attempt. Part of the prize was two years' study in Italy.

A few streets away, the theatre where Harriet was appearing closed with no warning. Harriet's job disappeared overnight – as did the theatre manager, clutching the box-office receipts for the whole season. Harriet, unpaid for five months' work, was owed 7500 francs. She was broke. Hers was the only income to support her invalid sister and elderly mother, both of whom travelled with her and depended on her entirely. To raise money for Harriet, a number of very distinguished fellow artists organised a benefit concert, planned for 28 November. One of the stars was the famous Italian ballerina Maria

The most famous bass of his generation, particularly acclaimed for his interpretation of comic roles, Luigi Lablache sang at the benefit concert for Harriet Smithson.

Taglioni, who had captivated audiences with her grace and beauty. Another was the distinguished bass Luigi Lablache, one of the highest-paid singers of his day. He had a formidable stage presence, and a paunch to match. Maria Malibran, the celebrated operatic prima donna, planned to appear, but a few days before the concert she fell ill, and it had to be postponed to the following week, 5 December.

Once again, fate was to intervene; 5 December was also to be the date of the first performance of the Fantastic Symphony. It was rumoured that Berlioz had chosen that date simply to spite Harriet, to fix a counter-attraction and to steal the public from her charity concert, but that seems highly unlikely. However badly Berlioz was behaving towards his old flame, he was not to know that one of the stars would be indisposed at the last minute and that Harriet's concert would have to be switched to another date. If indeed there had been any backstage rivalry, neither event suffered; Harriet's concert grossed 15,000 francs, and the première of Berlioz's Fantastic Symphony was cheered to the rafters.

With the triumph of the symphony ringing in his ears, Berlioz reluctantly turned his back on Paris and his beloved Camille, leaving his fiancée for the Villa Medici, his base in Italy during his Prix de Rome sojourn. When he arrived there he was worried that there was no letter from Camille awaiting him. The weeks passed, and he did some sightseeing, but still no word from Camille. Then, at last, a letter arrived. He had been jilted. His fiancée, the adorable Camille, had thrown him over to marry a wealthy, middle-aged piano manufacturer, Joseph Pleyel, head of a very famous and prosperous business. His dreams of love shattered, his ego crushed, Berlioz plotted revenge and worked out a detailed and absurd plan.

He would leave Italy and return to France, dressed as a lady's maid. Having gained admittance to Camille's house on the pretext of delivering a letter, he would draw a pistol from the folds of his skirt and shoot Pleyel and Camille's mother. With them out of the way, he would confront Camille and blast her head off too. Documented in his memoirs is the fact that he ordered the maid's costume from a French milliner and loaded a pair of double-barrelled pistols. For good measure he went to an apothecary and bought poison – laudanum and strychnine – in case the pistols misfired and to end his own life when the dreadful deed was done. But however crazy his imagination, Berlioz was not completely mad – at least not twenty-four hours a day; while hatching this nefarious plot, he calmly and rationally tidied up the manuscript of the Fantastic Symphony and sent a fair copy to the conductor, Habeneck, to make certain he had a place reserved in posterity. With that task out of the way, he headed for Paris.

At Genoa he realised that his luggage – complete with murder weapons and maid's costume – had gone astray when he'd changed coaches. Undaunted, he obtained replacement props and disguise, but by this time even the police in Sardinia had grown suspicious, not without reason, faced with a demented Frenchman, kitted out with guns, poison and a French maid's uniform. They sent him packing and on a precipitous mountain pass Berlioz contemplated suicide. Indeed, when he reached Nice, he tried to drown himself – just a little bit – and was fished out of the sea, coughing and spluttering. By then he had had enough and gave up the idea of slaughtering the Camille household. The balmy atmosphere of the South of France worked its magic on him. He started composing again and returned to Rome for another year's study.

Ideally, that is where the story should end. But there was to be another chapter, and a bitterly sad one when Fate once more intervened. When he had returned to Paris from Italy, there was to be a second performance of his Fantastic Symphony, on 9 December 1832. The dashing young Franz Liszt was in the audience along with an astonishing collection of Romantic poets, performers and musicians. Frédéric Chopin was present on that occasion, as was another brilliant virtuoso, Paganini, one of the greatest violinists of all time and a devoted admirer of Berlioz. Indeed, all the great and famous of Parisian society seem to have been there: Chopin's mistress George Sand (like everyone else in the audience she knew all the intimate details of Berlioz's infatuation for Harriet); next to her was the great

Franz Liszt. (Ingres, detail)

Victor Hugo, surrounded by the literary lions of Romantic poetry – Alfred de Vigny, Heinrich Heine, Alexandre Dumas and Théophile Gautier. But all eyes turned in one direction, as a woman quietly entered one of the boxes. It was Harriet Smithson. 'Poor young man,' she said, as Berlioz took his seat. 'I expect he has forgotten me. At least, I hope he has.'

Berlioz idealised her as much as ever, describing Harriet as 'the Juliet, the Ophelia, for whom my heart is searching. If I could only drink from the cup of joy and sorrow which true love offers, and then, one autumn night, lulled by the north wind on some wild heath, to lie in her arms and sleep a deep, last sleep'. Five years had elapsed since he had first set eyes on her, and in all that time they had never actually met. The day after the concert, Harriet sent him a message of congratulations and he seized the opportunity to meet her in person, conscious of having maligned her during his flirtation with Camille. Despite opposition from their families, they eventually married. For a time they were happy together. Harriet bore him a son whom he adored. But within a few years their marriage was in trouble.

Harriet's career was virtually over. She tried to run her own theatrical company in Paris, but she was a hopeless business woman.

Not even the most charismatic of today's pop stars can rival the fame and adoration that Franz Liszt, shown here in caricature, enjoyed. A brilliant pianist, Liszt also was a fine orchestral conductor. His thirteen symphonic poems for orchestra explore a variety of musical structures and the piano pieces he wrote in his old age anticipate the changes in traditional techniques that were later codified by Schoenberg and others.

Indeed, she could speak only a few words of French. She and Berlioz communicated in pidgin French. At times they were desperately poor. Berlioz earned virtually nothing from his compositions. He was constantly dipping into what little he earned from journalism in order to promote concerts of his own music. Although he was an excellent writer – everything he wrote is wonderfully readable – journalism was time-consuming and poorly paid, and now he had a wife and child to support, plus Harriet's mother and invalid sister. Harriet became increasingly demoralised. A once-great actress, her looks gone, she drank more and more and Berlioz travelled abroad increasingly, conducting in Germany, Austria, England and Russia. In the end he left her for a singer, and not even a good one at that. Berlioz's much-loved son left home to join the navy.

Harriet's last years were intensely sad. A series of strokes paralysed her and robbed her of speech. Berlioz continued to send her money and, at the end, visited her constantly, nursing her as best he could. She was fifty-three when she died and even after her death the irony of that first vision of the young Shakespearian actress persisted, as he recounted in his memoirs:

Some years later, the little cemetery in Montmartre where she had been buried, was to be demolished and her remains had to be moved. The coffin, though ten years in the ground, was still intact; only the lid had decayed from damp. Instead of lifting out the whole coffin, the grave-digger wrenched at the rotting planks, which came away with a hideous crack, exposing the coffin's contents. The grave-digger bent down and, with his two hands, picked up the head, already parted from the body – the ungarlanded, withered head of 'poor Ophelia'.

The role of the orchestra in Wagner's music is raised to that of protagonist; it underlines the action, anticipates what is to come and reminds us of earlier episodes in the story, depicting not only the emotions but also the dramatic significance of inanimate objects.

Whatever the story, whatever the facts or the fiction in Berlioz's recollections of events, and however much they did or did not influence the way he composed the work, it is the originality of the Fantastic Symphony that is fascinating. Clearly Berlioz wished the audience to respond to the personal and graphic aspect of his work. He wrote not one but four sets of programme notes, insisting they should be distributed amongst the audience: 'A young musician of extraordinary sensibility and abundant imagination, in the depths of despair because of hopeless love . . .' With hindsight we can see how Berlioz imposed this structure to 'signpost' the composition. But within those broad descriptions he manipulated and developed his basic musical theme – that *idée fixe* – and took its rhythmic and melodic details to build up larger paragraphs, as in a conventional symphony. This idea of thematic transformation was to become a stan-

Like Liszt, Wagner and Mahler, Strauss was a fine conductor – and he gained an assured knowledge of orchestral effects and instrumental sonorities; also like them he was often the subject of caricature, accused of writing strident and psychotic music.

dard technique of the nineteenth century as the traditional form of the symphony spawned other progeny, most notably the symphonic poem, in the work of Franz Liszt, Richard Strauss and many other composers. The idea of thematic transformation permeated the music dramas of Richard Wagner, and it was to become a flexible and useful method of construction.

Berlioz's most important innovation, however, was to regard the orchestration of his ideas not as icing on the cake but as the essence of the music itself. He thought instinctively in terms of the specific tone-colour of orchestral instruments. Indeed, he was the author of

a massive compendium of orchestral effects, a fascinating textbook. Yet he himself could play nothing more than a few notes on a penny whistle and one or two chords on the Spanish guitar. Unlike almost every major composer before him, he was no keyboard player. Consequently his imagination was never confined to thinking only in terms of ten fingers on a piano. On the contrary, his orchestration breaks all the rules: high shrieking violins; deep trombones and tubas growling like animals; batteries of kettledrums, played by several players at the same time, making up a chord.

In this way, his music becomes intensely descriptive, especially in the movement from the Fantastic Symphony entitled Dream of a Witches' Sabbath. It is as specifically descriptive as the background music to any 'video nasty' and rather more skilful. It is really a symphonic poem in its own right, illustrating specific events bar by bar. Our hero, that 'impressionable young composer', has been executed for killing his beloved. Now, a witness at his own funeral, he observes the final mockery as 'a fearful crowd of spectres, sorcerers, and monsters of every kind congregate for his burial':

Unearthly sounds [wrote Berlioz], groans, shrieks of laughter, distant cries . . . The melody of the beloved is heard, but it has lost its character of nobility and reserve. Instead, it is corrupted into an ignoble dance tune, trivial and grotesque. It is she who comes to the Sabbath. A shout of joy greets her arrival. She joins in the diabolical orgy. The funeral knell, and a burlesque of the Dies Irae [the famous chant from the Requiem Mass of the Catholic Church] combine with the Witches' Dance.

Elaborate mechanisms were sometimes required to realise Wagner's poetic visions on stage. These are the swimming carriages for the Rhine Maidens, used in 1876.

— 119 —

The conventional orchestra pit was unacceptable to Wagner (who can be seen peeking through the cubby-hole in the centre of this illustration of a rehearsal of his opera *Parsifal*). His design for the opera-house at Bayreuth shielded the instruments so as to transform the acoustic balance between singers and orchestra.

Louis Jullien conducting a concert at Covent Garden in 1846. 'The Paganini of the Alps' was one of the most successful conductors of the nineteenth century. He conducted Beethoven with a jewelled baton handed to him on a silver salver, and came to be regarded as 'undoubtedly the first who directed the attention of the multitude to the Classical composers. He broke down the barriers and let in the crowd.'

This is powerful stuff – and nearly a century before Stravinsky's *Rite of Spring.*

From the outset Berlioz establishes the mood of suspense – a shimmering, barely audible chord, and then sounds which imitate a flurry of witches descending from the sky. This provokes the barking of a dog and the hoot of an owl in the night. Even today, such vivid

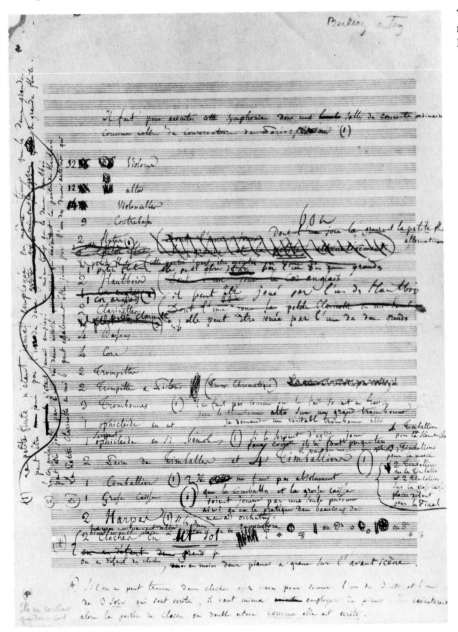

The title-page of the manuscript of Berlioz's Fantastic Symphony.

orchestration is both effective and bizarre, although our ears have become jaded by horror movies and background music. If we imagine ourselves in Berlioz's audience, however, we see instantly that those sounds – totally without precedent – must have scared the daylights out of the listeners. Berlioz could not have copied them from anybody else, for the simple reason that nobody – not even in the opera-house – ever had the audacity to conjure up anything so original. Likewise, the 'voicing' of trombone chords defies all tradition. Berlioz accompanies the travesty of the Beloved theme with two kettledrums and a bass-drum – a demented, satanic parody. The arrival at the Witches' Sabbath of the beloved is greeted with a raucous, cackling braying from the entire orchestra, and the melody is repeated with an accompaniment of bassoons – bubbling and gurgling like a witches' cauldron.

Then Berlioz deals his trump card. There is a moment of stillness. A distant church bell signals the Black Mass to begin. We hear the

A contemporary caricature of Hector Berlioz unleashing his unprecedented orchestral effects.

Latin chant, the Dies Irae – recognisable instantly to every member of the Catholic audience – interspersed with the parody of the Beloved theme. The satanic ritual takes over and the theme is transformed yet again, treated as a fugue (but not in the least academic), a frenzied witches' dance, combined in counterpoint with the Dies Irae theme. Then, in another master-stroke, comes a complete change of sonority as Berlioz instructs the violins and the violas to turn their bows round the wrong way and to play not with the hair but the wood – the dry, eerie rattle of skeletons dancing. The work builds to a climax with a virtuoso display of drumming and the full power of a massive orchestra. From first note to last, every bar of the Fantastic Symphony bears the mark of total originality and daring. It is impossible to think of any other composer who would so much as dream of taking that sort of risk, and who would have possessed the outrageous genius to carry it off.

Throughout his life Berlioz was obsessed with the expressive potential of sound: 'Music should be free, imperious, all-conquering. I want it to seize everything,' he said. Such a resolute personality, holding such uncompromising views about his art, struck many of his contemporaries as autocratic, arrogant and aloof. Ernest Legouvé, poet and lifelong friend of Berlioz and the dedicatee of the Benvenuto Cellini Overture, described him as

an extraordinary mixture of enthusiasm and mockery; a mind that you could never predict; conversation that had you constantly on the alert by its very changeability; long brooding silences, with lowered eyes and a glance that seemed to plumb unimaginable depths. Then a sudden recovery of spirits, a stream of brilliant, amusing or touching remarks, bursts of Homeric laughter, and a delight like a child's.

Van Gogh, a few years later, wrote of Berlioz: 'Perhaps one day everyone will have a neurosis. . .'

6
'Something out of Nothing'

In the Fantastic Symphony Hector Berlioz, a Frenchman, had taken the tradition of Viennese Classicism as it had developed in the symphonies of Haydn, Mozart, Beethoven and Schubert, and within a year or two of Beethoven's death turned the whole thing on its head. But the long-cherished abstract symphonic principles of Classicism did not simply disappear with the advent of Romanticism. One man who revered those techniques, who understood them and breathed new life into them, making them his own, was Johannes Brahms.

At various times Brahms has been called conservative, reactionary and stuffy. 'A throw-back from a bygone age,' said his contemporaries. 'Has he no idea of the "Music of the Future"? – the achievements of progressives like Berlioz, Liszt and Wagner?'

Brahms was a young man when he started work on his First Symphony. From first note to last it was to take him the best part of twenty years to complete. When it appeared it was referred to dismissively as 'Beethoven's Tenth'. 'Brahms,' said the critic and songwriter Hugo Wolf, 'writes symphonies regardless of what happened in between.' Hugo Wolf was particularly vicious about Brahms's Fourth Symphony:

He could never rise above mediocrity. But such nothingness, such hollowness, such mousy obsequiousness as this has never yet been revealed so alarmingly in any of Brahms's works. The 'Art of Composing Without Ideas' has decidedly found in Brahms one of its worthiest representatives. Like God Almighty, Brahms understands the trick of creating something out of nothing.

Tchaikovsky was even more forthright, calling Brahms 'a giftless bastard'.

To us, such criticism seems ludicrous, however much Brahms chose to swim against the tide. In his symphonies, as in all his music, Brahms was his own man. In his formal control, his harmonic language, the integrity of his materials, and in dozens of other ways, Brahms was a conservative working in a Classical tradition. When Wagner and Berlioz favoured bigger, more lavish, instrumental textures, Brahms was content to use a conventional, Beethoven-sized, relatively small orchestra.

Brahms was born in 1833 and died in 1897, aged sixty-three. Everything he wrote displays the most superb craftsmanship and a traditional, classical sense of order and design. Most portraits show him after he had grown a flowing beard. But as a young man he cut a dashingly handsome figure and was much in demand as a conductor by choirs of young ladies. They fell at his feet, but he remained a bachelor all his life.

When Brahms was twenty he met Robert Schumann, an influential critic and composer. He set Brahms on his career, praising him to the skies. Three years later Schumann died and Brahms fell in love with

Above: Brahms as a boy (Carpentias). By the age of ten he had become known in Hamburg as a formidable pianist.

Left: Brahms as a young man.

Robert Schumann (top) was quick to appreciate Brahms's enormous talent and did much to launch him on his career.

Clara Schumann nursed her husband through increasing bouts of depression and his last pathetic months in a madhouse.

his widow, Clara. Fourteen years older than Brahms, she was the first truly internationally-renowned woman pianist. Somehow she managed to bring up her seven children and, at the same time, pursue her career as a concert pianist. Today, in a different world, in a different age, she and Brahms might well have married. But Clara's life was dedicated to the memory of her husband and to her own career. Brahms respected Clara's musicianship as much as he loved her as a person, turning to her constantly for advice, sending her his new compositions, seeking her criticism and guidance. They maintained an enduring friendship all their lives. There were other romantic attachments, mainly to singers; but composition was his life and he was his own fiercest critic, ruthlessly tearing up pages of manuscript, or entire compositions, if he was not totally happy with them, or if he considered them in the least immature or unworthy. Consequently he left behind no uncompleted works or pieces that demonstrate indecision or lack of inspiration. This is why everything he left behind is so durable. His orchestral music, particularly, has implanted itself firmly in the concert-hall repertoire. Despite changes of fashion, his music remains a challenge to play, but is ever fruitful, ever rewarding. His four symphonies are staples of the repertoire, and rightly so. But he had reached the age of forty before he felt confident enough to present his First Symphony to the public, and he was not in the least disheartened when critics compared its song-like finale to the last movement of Beethoven's Choral Symphony. 'Any donkey can see that,' he said.

His musical personality is rich in lyricism, expressiveness and instrumental warmth, and possesses a most distinctive tone of voice. Brahms's music, like that of Schubert or Chopin, is instantly recognisable; its powerful rhythmic and harmonic style resembles nobody else's. Moreover, Brahms has a highly developed sense of proportion, an impeccable sense of formal structure and architectural shape. It is the combination of such qualities that gives his music such unique powers of endurance.

Of all his contemporaries, Brahms had the most scholarly, sensitive and sympathetic knowledge of the music of the past. This was no mere amateur interest. From childhood, he loved the music of Bach, Handel and other Baroque composers such as the French keyboard virtuoso François Couperin. As a boy in Hamburg he was always hunting around antiquarian bookshops or digging out old manuscripts from the city library to copy and study. He particularly loved to mull over instances where composers of distinction had broken the 'rules' of formal counterpoint. These he jotted down not to show his cleverness but to see how – faced with certain technical problems – Bach and others had got themselves out of tight corners. This great enthusiasm for early music stayed with him, and as a musicologist he edited it for publication.

The techniques of the past also inspired him as a composer: theme and variations, fugue, sonata-form and so on. As far as his contemporaries were concerned, such ideas were utterly out of date, although to Brahms they came completely naturally. He had an innate need for the discipline of form. Consequently, the art of taking a theme and writing a set of variations upon it held a particular fascination for him, as it had for Beethoven. It gave him great fluency in handling symphonic material; it taught him how to reveal, time and again, fresh aspects of a musical theme; to organise a wealth of detail within a large-scale, clearly perceived framework. That quality is abundantly demonstrated in his Fourth Symphony, with its massive architecture, a quality that gives his music ageless appeal, placing it – like the music of Bach, the piano concertos of Mozart, and the quartets of Beethoven – above and beyond any changes in public taste.

Such an achievement is quite extraordinary when one considers that Brahms never went in for anything that might be called flashy or gimmicky. His orchestration is a prime example. On his own admission Brahms did not think naturally in terms of orchestral colour. At a time when composers such as Berlioz, Liszt and Wagner were exploring ever bigger, ever more voluptuous orchestral sonorities, Brahms was content – even in his mature works – with the orchestra as Beethoven and Schubert had left it more than half a century earlier. Not for Johannes Brahms the extra brass, the additional woodwind, or the glittering impact of the percussion department. Nevertheless, Brahms's orchestration is totally personal and such is his mastery of musical thought over mere orchestral effect that his popularity in the record shops and concert-halls exceeds that of such brilliant orchestrators as Richard Strauss, Rimsky-Korsakov and Ravel.

Unlike so many nineteenth-century artists, Brahms did not pour out his philosophy by writing lengthy explanations; neither did he theorise about how music should or should not be composed. Unlike Wagner, for example, he was not in the least interested in the fusion of painting, literature, music and all the other arts. Indeed, Brahms loathed the idea. As a result he dissociated himself from the influential

and 'progressive' ideals of Liszt and his son-in-law Richard Wagner
– the New German School, as it was known. His own inclinations
were diametrically opposed. Where Liszt's harmony goes out on a
limb (anticipating the atonality associated with Schoenberg and the
Second Viennese School) Brahms is cautious. In using a relatively
modest-sized orchestra, he knew precisely what sort of instrumen-
tation would most suitably clothe his musical thought. When he
thickens the orchestral texture, especially in richly voiced lower
instruments, it is never from ineptitude but because the particular
sound is an integral expression of what he has to say, as when he
divides the violas and cellos to get that Brahmsian warmth and richness of sound. His inventiveness is not the sort that proclaims itself
from the rooftops. It is far more subtle; he entrusts, for example, a
melody to the violas, played in the normal way with bows, but with
the notes of the tune doubled by plucked violins.

In an age of outspoken egoists, Brahms was basically a reserved
man, although he could put on a sociable air of *bonhomie* when he
chose. He let his music stand on its own merits. Against his will he
found himself chosen as the symbol of the anti-Wagnerian faction
in the musical world. The battle of words that raged between the
Wagnerites and the Brahmsians seems ludicrous today. When the dust
had settled, it was another composer, Arnold Schoenberg, who put
the matter into perspective. He wrote an essay entitled 'Brahms the
Progressive' where he demonstrated that modern music owed as much
to Brahms as it did to Wagner – an attitude that would have been
dismissed as preposterous in Brahms's lifetime and for years
afterwards.

In many countries Brahms's symphonies needed time to find an
established place in the repertoire. André Previn, for example, tells
how his father as a young man in Germany was a member of a Brahms
fan club, an organisation to help promote Brahms's music. In 1900,
when Symphony Hall was being built in Boston, Massachusetts, the
joke was that the exit signs over the doors should say 'Exit in Case
of Brahms'. His music was regarded as turgid, difficult to understand,
and old-fashioned. In his years as music critic, George Bernard Shaw
could never resist twisting the knife:

18th June 1890. My temper was not improved by Brahms's Symphony in E Minor
(No. 4). He takes an essentially commonplace theme and gives it a strange air by
dressing it in the most elaborate and far-fetched harmonies. Strip off the euphemism
from these symphonies, and you will find a string of incomplete dance and ballad

tunes, following each other with no more organic coherence than a succession of passing images reflected in a shop window in Piccadilly during any twenty minutes in the day. Brahms's enormous gift of music is paralleled by nothing on earth but Mr Gladstone's gift of words; it is a verbosity which outfaces its own commonplaceness by dint of sheer magnitude. He is insufferably tedious. His symphonies are endured as sermons are endured.

Remarks such as those tell us more about GBS than they do about Brahms. Clearly, Shaw found it incomprehensible that Brahms should choose resolutely to work in traditional forms – theme and variations, fugue and similar abstract structures – where musical inventiveness is of the essence. In such forms there is no Wagnerian plot or sub-plot to provide a story-line; there is no Irish actress – à la Berlioz – to provide inspiration. To us Brahms is a composer whose music is the embodiment of the Germanic symphonic tradition, that ability to create an entire musical edifice from half a dozen snippets of notes and rhythms.

For years it seemed that Beethoven, in carrying such an idea to extraordinary lengths (as in the first movement of his Fifth Symphony, for example), had exhausted all possibility of further endeavour on such lines. The Ninth Symphony had been seen as a bridgehead into new territory, where the different arts combined. In Brahms, however, we have a figure of paramount importance in the continued development of the Classical idea. Looking at the broad spectrum of 'the symphony', we can see how different composers at different times have taken the notion of orchestral music designed on similar architectural lines, and used it to their own ends. From its early growth in the eighteenth century, its maturity in Haydn and Mozart and its violent transformation in the imagination of Beethoven, the symphony had changed out of all recognition, bearing little resemblance to the compositions of Mannheim composers such as Stamitz. Berlioz, a composer who revered Beethoven, changed the contours yet again, with the expression of a wild, tortured, impulsive, fantastic imagination. But even his Fantastic Symphony remains very securely a symphony, however much we – and Berlioz too for that matter – choose to read into the programme notes.

If we look at the symphonies of Brahms, we can see why composers of every period persist in writing music of symphonic proportions. It is because the symphony, unlike many other musical disciplines, cannot be faked. Other forms of musical expression – opera, ballet, choral works, concertos – can, in a way, cheat. In an opera or a ballet, there is the scenery, the story, the staging, lighting and costumes to distract the audience. In a concerto there is always the charisma of the soloist or the brilliance of the playing to make up for the intellectual shortcomings of the piece. But in a symphony (as in the string quartet which has a parallel origin) the only thing to be judged is the quality of the composer himself and his ability to develop his musical ideas. Development is the essence of symphonic thought — the process whereby germs of ideas expand, mature and flourish according to the skill of the composer.

This quality is evident throughout Brahms's Fourth Symphony. The work starts with a gentle see-sawing phrase on the violins. At one stage Brahms toyed with the idea of putting a few bars' introduction in front, but decided against it. Instead, he starts straight in with the main theme, a drop of a third and a rise of a sixth. This is immediately balanced by a similar pattern. Each element in the phrase starts on a weak beat, which propels it forward, and the swaying off-beat feeling is emphasised by the woodwind, which also echoes the melody, and by the accompaniment in the lower strings, an undercurrent that rises and falls.

He repeats the theme with a wealth of decorative detail, simultaneously interweaving several versions of the same melody. He introduces a new idea, a muted fanfare, and then suddenly we are in the middle of a lush, romantic melody accompanied by a rhythm that can only be described as a tango. Then Brahms magically interrupts the flow of movement, freezes the harmony, and holds us in suspense as distant fanfares approach. He develops the idea instantly just as he develops every musical idea the moment he presents it. Indeed, so rich are Brahms's powers of invention that he makes nonsense of the traditional dividing lines of a symphony. Barely ten or twelve dozen bars into the work and long before we reach what the textbooks call the 'development section', everything we encounter has been in itself an extension, a transformation, a realisation — a development — of something else.

When we do finally reach the 'development section', Brahms's imagination and intellectual skill take flight. Picking on the briefest fragments of melody, he conjures up a passage full of ingenuity. He combines his ideas with mirror-images of themselves and turns them into canons which are again mirrored. Like *Three Blind Mice*, canons are tunes that work when sung by several people, one after the other, separated only by a few beats; but they are also *mirror* canons, and when one voice goes up, the other goes down. That, as any composition student will confirm, is a difficult enough puzzle to work out. But Brahms adds yet another canon on top of that. The interesting thing about a passage of such bewildering intellectual skill is that only the most dedicated professional musician needs to dig into its subtleties. When you listen to that section as a member of an audience, it is over in a flash – ten or twenty seconds. Judged purely as a musical climax, irrespective of the intellectual subtlety that lies behind it, it is still an impressive ten or twenty seconds. Brahms also achieves his effects by simpler means, for example in the way he brings back the opening theme, almost without us realising it.

Every note in this work displays a symphonic intellect of immense power, a composer ranking beside Beethoven, Bach and Mozart. Yet for years Brahms shied away from committing himself publicly as a symphonist, conscious always of the shadow of Beethoven. 'I shall never compose a symphony,' he wrote to Clara Schumann when he was in his late thirties. 'You cannot have any idea what it's like to hear such a giant marching behind you.' That is a daunting burden to have on one's shoulders. In Brahms's case – more than other Romantic artists – it made symphonic writing even more of a challenge because he revered the Beethoven idea of musical development so deeply and was drawn quite naturally to think and create in terms of craftsmanship. One should not pretend that Brahms's contemporaries took their job any less seriously, but they felt drawn to different methods of expression. When Brahms, in the final movement of this symphony, adopted a Baroque technique – the *passacaglia*, a set of variations over a repeated theme – it must have seemed, to the avant-garde, sheer madness.

The theme came from a cantata by Bach but this was no mere borrowing. When Brahms adopted traditional techniques it was because they sparked off in him his own inexhaustible powers of invention. The finale is based entirely on an eight-bar theme, presented with authority, for this is the moment in the symphony where Brahms introduces the rich sonority of the trombones for the first time. The theme, in one guise or another, recurs some thirty-one times without modulating to a different key and without any bridge-passages or interludes. It appears alternately in high, middle and low 'voices'.

In other words, Brahms has intentionally imposed severe constraints upon himself. Within these apparently narrow confines, so resourceful and ingenious is he that he builds music of great force and grandeur. Indeed, the finale is so full of contrast and inventive-ness that the technical mastery takes second place to the intensity of feeling. Musically, in all sorts of ways, there are many parallels between the finale and the three earlier movements. These parallels are so numerous that they cannot be explained away as mere coincidence. Clearly, Brahms, with a marvellous architectural sense, places as much weight on the finale as he does on the opening movement.

Brahms with Johann Strauss II (left) in 1894.

Earlier generations of symphonists — Haydn, Schubert, Mendelssohn, for example — often regarded the finale as a light-hearted, perhaps boisterous conclusion, full of rollicking good tunes. But for Brahms it was a culmination — a majestic and comprehensive summing up — of what had gone before. In a finale of this length, lasting nearly a quarter of an hour, it is important to create areas of light and shade, to provide moments of repose, especially after opening the movement with solemn trombone chords. Brahms provides this by grouping his variations into contrasting moods, longer paragraphs, before bringing us back into the heroic mood established at the start. Above all else, what unifies this finale — giving a sense of onward propulsion — is the way Brahms makes one rhythmic idea flow into the next. The abiding impression is not how clever Brahms has been, or how brilliant and technically ingenious, but how honest and how beautiful, since he never tries to show off, or to impress with his technical skill. For Brahms, impeccable craftsmanship is part and parcel of what he has to say. The emotion and the technique are one and the same thing and could not be expressed in any other way.

In an age of Romanticism that type of unity eluded many composers — hence the symphonic poem where the emotional ebb and flow of the story helped dictate the structure of the music, propelling us from one episode to the next. But in Brahms's Fourth Symphony we have an orchestral work (the last purely orchestral work he was to compose) of great structure, and of central importance in the development of the main symphonic tradition.

7
'The Most Russian of us All'

In the last half of the nineteenth century, composers such as Richard Strauss and Hector Berlioz took orchestration and the transformation of themes to a point where music could be as pictorial as any painting. In the world of opera, the music dramas of Richard Wagner used thematic transformation not merely to identify characters in the drama but to chart emotional changes, to label inanimate objects and, from moment to moment, to commentate and underline thoughts, feelings, aspirations and memories.

In its size, variety, flexibility and expressiveness of its tone-colours the symphony orchestra had become a rich and infinitely subtle palette. The virtuosity of the playing, the ability of a composer such as Richard Strauss to impersonate everything from a flock of sheep (bleating trumpets) to an erection (French horns rampant) became legendary. At the same time, voluptuous harmonies, spacious melodies and the power of the modern symphony orchestra established a richness of sound that even today, a century on, we still call 'romantic'. It is the sound that conjures up the grand days of Hollywood epics, the splendour of the Bolshoi, the soaring violins and vibrant counter-melodies, the anguish of *Gone with the Wind*, and the longing of *Brief Encounter*.

The origin of this category of music can be traced back to the beginning of the nineteenth century, to the nocturnes of Frédéric Chopin, and even earlier to figures like the Irishman John Field, whose lyrical talent as a composer founded a tradition of melodic Romanticism.

Much later in the nineteenth century it was the Russian composer Tchaikovsky whose melodies, self-contained and complete in themselves, summed up that style – expressive, romantic and heartfelt. Tchaikovsky, for years, has been frowned on by the musical establishment for the most illogical of reasons – because he is a truly popular composer; because his music is direct, honest, tuneful, and highly emotional; and because millions of people who would never have the confidence to attend a 'symphony concert' will happily go in coachloads to a 'Tchaikovsky night' to listen to the *1812* Overture, *Swan Lake*, and 'the' Tchaikovsky piano concerto. What is the magic in his music? Why do we respond to it as we do?

Tchaikovsky was born in 1840, the son of a mining engineer. As a child he was often moody and easily reduced to tears. Today a child psychologist might label him 'emotionally disturbed'. He was devoted to his mother and utterly distraught when, at the age of ten, he was parted from her and sent to join the preparatory class of the law school in St Petersburg. At nineteen he completed his course in the school of jurisprudence and took a post as a clerk in the ministry of justice. And so Tchaikovsky was in his mid-twenties before he turned seriously to music. Soon he was obsessed with operatic and dramatic

Tchaikovsky (Kuznetsov, detail). The original 'Mighty Fistful' of Russian nationalist composers often criticised his music as too westernised, yet Tchaikovsky assimilated with great skill the inflections and rhythms of Russian folk-music into his symphonies and ballet scores.

subjects. His formal conservatoire training at St Petersburg was firmly based on the musical tradition of Western Europe but his true nature, he always insisted, was Russian, not only in his occasional use of folk-song but in his deep absorption in Russian life and ways of thought. His natural gift for writing beautiful, introspective melodies gave his music lasting appeal, and it is this genius for lyricism, and the technical mastery of orchestration he eventually developed, that quickly established his popularity in Russia and abroad.

Above all he had a flair for writing the most enchanting ballet music, especially waltzes; even in his symphonies the world of the dance is never far away. For this reason they have been criticised as being 'nothing but a sequence of tunes, stitched together with the seams showing'. True, his symphonies are not crafted with the same architectural qualities found in the symphonies of Brahms; but Tchaikovsky hated the music of Brahms anyway. Indeed, in his diary of 9 October 1886, he indelicately referred to Brahms as 'a giftless bastard'. 'It annoys me,' he wrote, 'that Brahms, with his self-inflated mediocrity, is hailed as a genius . . . Brahms's music is chaotic and absolutely empty, dried-up stuff.' This smacks of more than just a touch of jealousy; Tchaikovsky was always conscious that the structural control required to move effortlessly and inevitably in a symphony from one musical idea to the next was never his strongest point. His emotion – many would say emotionalism – ruled his head.

As a student, Tchaikovsky had become increasingly introverted and felt an oppressive sense of guilt about his homosexuality. In a desperate attempt to convince people of his respectability, he let it be known that he was thinking of getting married. He was thirty-three and had started work on his opera *Eugene Onegin*, when he received what amounted to a fan letter from a girl called Antonina, declaring her love for him. It was a crazy letter and Tchaikovsky could not even recollect meeting her. She threatened suicide if he refused to see her. When they met he told her firmly, but not unkindly, that it was impossible for him to love her. There the matter might have ended. However, he became obsessed by the sequence in *Eugene Onegin* he was currently working on, where Onegin heartlessly rejects Tatiana. This made Tchaikovsky reconsider his own rejection of Antonina. Impetuously, and within a week of their meeting, they were engaged – although he had tried to make it clear to her that any physical relationship between them was out of the question. A month later they were married. Inevitably the marriage was a tragedy. They

Tchaikovsky and Antonina.

parted almost immediately. Tchaikovsky had a complete nervous breakdown and made a pathetic attempt at suicide.

Even more bizarre was his friendship with Nadezhda von Meck. She was a wealthy widow who had been impressed by some of his music a few years previously and had helped him financially. It was the start of an extraordinary relationship that was to last fourteen years, during which all personal contact between them was avoided. Their relationship was solely by correspondence. On the two occasions when they accidentally met they hurried past each other without speaking. Each regarded the other as a fantasy figure, unspoilt by the disenchantment of reality.

Madame von Meck granted Tchaikovsky an annuity of 6000 roubles, a substantial income that continued even when his success

Madame von Meck, a
wealthy widow, subsidised
Tchaikovsky for fourteen
years; their only contact was
by correspondence, although
her son married
Tchaikovsky's niece.

brought him royalties. On top of that, the Tsar granted him a pension of 3000 roubles for life. Few composers in their lifetime enjoyed similar success. His compositions were greeted enthusiastically in America and Europe. His music was fashionable and tuneful. He was in great demand as a conductor. In the academic world honours were showered upon him. He was elected to the Académie française. The University of Cambridge conferred on him an honorary doctorate of music – in a ceremony where it also honoured the composers Saint-Saëns, Max Bruch, Grieg and Verdi's librettist, Boito.

However, in a way that is typically Russian, the greater Tchaikovsky's success, the greater his depression. He was not yet fifty-three when Kuznetsov painted his well-known portrait (page 135), yet he looks twenty years older, although the composer's brother, Modest, always claimed it was the best and truest likeness. In February 1893 he wrote that he had started work 'on another symphony – this time a programme symphony', a composition that contained an underlying story, emotional or factual.

Tchaikovsky in the academic
robes of the University of
Cambridge.

But [said the composer] the programme shall remain a mystery for everyone. They may guess as they please, but the symphony will be called merely 'A Programme Symphony' [No. 6]. The underlying programme is totally personal to me, deeply subjective, and I often wept profusely as I settled down to write the sketches. The composition is going with such intensity, with such speed, that I had the first movement ready in less than four days, and the others have taken shape in my head. As regards the form of the piece, there will be in this symphony a great deal that is new. Among other things, the finale will not be a noisy *Allegro*, but – on the contrary – a very protracted *Adagio*.

In a statement that was to take on a bitter irony as the months passed he noted he was in better spirits. Believing he had shaken off the depression that had haunted him, he added touchingly, 'You can't conceive what bliss it is for me to be convinced that my time is not yet over and that I am still able to work. Of course it is possible that I am mistaken, but I don't think so.'

Although composing the symphony took him only a few weeks, working out the orchestration gave him enormous trouble, which for him was unusual. 'Twenty years ago,' he said, 'I rushed along at full speed without giving it a thought, and it turned out well. Now I've become timorous and unsure of myself. I spent the whole of today sitting over two pages; somehow everything is turning out not quite as I'd thought.' He completed the score towards the end of August, saying the comparative slowness of the orchestration had not been caused by any decline in his skill but was the result 'of my having become a deal stricter with myself . . . I am very proud of the symphony. It's the most sincere of all my works, and I regard it as the best of all my compositions'.

He conducted the first performance at St Petersburg on 28 October. The orchestral players, he said, seemed lacking in enthusiasm, but the première was well enough received by the audience and critics, if not with an ovation as jubilant as he had become used to. The morning after the première, his brother Modest found him trying to decide on a title. Tchaikovsky no longer felt it was satisfactory just to give the symphony a number, or to call it merely 'A Programme Symphony', without giving away what the programme conveyed. Modest suggested 'Tragic', because of the work's profound pessimism and the expressive extremes of its dynamics, from tumultuous loudness to the quietest whisp of barely audible sound, and because of the intense grief and desolation that dominated the piece. But 'Tragic' was not exactly the right word to describe the mood of suffering and pathos. 'Pathétique' – his brother's next suggestion – was acceptable.

Stravinsky by Picasso (1920).

Unfortunately the English language has no equivalent. Pathetic has acquired an utterly different meaning and we have no single word that encapsulates the sense of anguish and sorrow established at the start of the piece.

The work opens with a lugubrious bassoon solo, painfully dragging its way notch by notch up the scale, the phrase falling back on itself with repeated sighs; nothing could be more Russian than the doom and gloom of such orchestral colours – the darkness of cellos and basses. Indeed, another composer, Igor Stravinsky, said, 'Tchaikovsky was the most Russian of us all.' After the slow introduction, the intensity of emotion remains in the music, even when the tempo quickens. When the skies brighten, so to speak, there is still that overpowering atmosphere of anguish as we encounter the rich romantic melody of the first movement. It is a theme of remarkable beauty and lyrical power. Yet the anguish is created by the simplest of devices; he makes the melody repeatedly fall back on itself. This sighing effect, as in the opening bars of the piece, is reinforced by harmony so intense that it is almost operatic – the tension placed always on the 'strong' beats. The music develops, taking the two notes of the 'sigh' (G down to F sharp) and spinning them into a passage of scales which Tchaikovsky then throws around the orchestra, and the 'sigh' is

Igor Stravinsky at the piano at a rehearsal of *The Firebird*.

worked into a (sort of) fugue. Then, once more, he drags us down into that deep Russian gloom of the beginning.

The second movement, a waltz, is unusual. Once again, the melody is based on the notes of the scale. But instead of the customary three beats in the bar, this waltz has five. Yet it is still a waltz and it floats as balletically as anything from *Swan Lake* or *The Nutcracker*.

It is the third movement of this symphony, however, that invariably has the audience sitting on the edge of their seats. This time the 'sigh' – the drop from one note to the one below – is dressed up into scampering passages for the violins, before it breaks into the march tune proper. With great skill – both as composer and as orchestrator – Tchaikovsky has composed one of the most blazingly effective moments in any symphony, with glorious climaxes, theatrical, colourful, balletic. The movement is all the more dramatic for being unashamedly honest, as is every note he put on paper. There is no trick in it; everything he wrote is technically immaculate, interesting to play, direct and appealing in its expressiveness. He wears his heart on his shoulder, yet he is so good at his job that he makes it all sound easy. It is actually not at all difficult to compose music that sounds complicated; but it takes a really intelligent composer to write music that sounds straightforward and, above all, inevitable.

Like it or not, when you listen to Tchaikovsky you start to feel the hairs on the back of your neck, and there is nothing you can do about it, because what he has written is irresistible.

In the fourth and final movement Tchaikovsky really bares his soul. It was audacious of him – courageous even – to end the symphony in a mood of such tragic pessimism, but from the initial conception of the symphony it is clear that is how he wanted it to end – not with a bang, not even with a whimper, but simply fading away to a mere wisp of sound. Tchaikovsky leaves no doubt in the minds of either players or conductors as to his intentions; this degree of quietness is marked in the heaviest of pencil in the manuscript. In music the *p* stands for piano; *pp* means pianissimo. Here Tchaikovsky doubles it up again – four of them. Even after that, he still resolutely marks a 'hairpin', a decrescendo floating away to nothing.

One of the theories about the 'meaning' of this work is that Tchaikovsky planned, in his last years, to write a symphony where the four movements depicted Youth, Love, Disappointment and Death. 'The ending,' he said, 'dies away.' With so little real knowledge of what was going on in Tchaikovsky's mind and heart, this work

The final bars of the symphony, after a diminuendo to *pppp*, die away to the merest wisp of sound.

remains an enigma. Commentators have been free to read into the composition whatever symbolism or interpretation suits them. The start of the last movement, again based on a scale, has never been convincingly explained. The effect on the *ear* of the listener is straightforward enough – the theme is dramatically presented on the violins. Yet the way the melody is *written* is baffling. Tchaikovsky alternates the notes of the tune between the two groups of violins – 'firsts' and 'seconds' – so that the melody, in a totally unconventional way, makes sense to the ear only when played by *both* groups of violins. From his original sketches we can see that he fretted over several different versions.

Why go to such extraordinary trouble? One explanation is that it was customary in those days for first and second violins to sit on opposite sides of the platform, and so – it is argued – Tchaikovsky intended a sort of stereophonic effect. But to go to such lengths seems

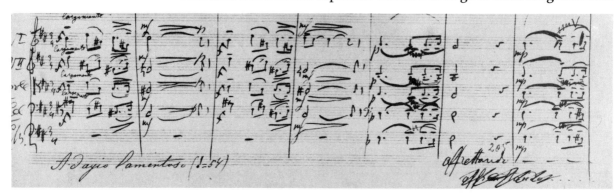

The opening theme of the last movement of the Symphony No. 6.

obsessive. Looked at as a melody, the line of notes played by the first violins makes no sense at all. Neither does the line of notes allotted to the seconds. Individually, both lines are awkward, unresolved, inconsequential, incomplete. Marry the two together, and they merge and complement each other perfectly. Had Sigmund Freud turned his attention to these few bars of music, he would surely have had a field-day. Even more curious is that when the passage returns later on, the very same notes are no longer broken up in that way, but are presented conventionally as a single, continuous melodic line, complete in itself, entrusted solely to the first violins.

Whatever the explanation, it is undeniable that Tchaikovsky was a lonely man with a burning need to communicate with others. As a homosexual in Russia at that time, he was guilty of the most grievous of sins. His marriage had been a disaster. Yet he was a deeply emotional man who poured out his heart in his music, and in this work in particular. To conclude the symphony in a mood of such deep pessimism was courageous of him. Audiences have firmly held views as to how a symphony should end: on a note of optimism, good-humour, jubilation or triumph. Indeed, had Tchaikovsky concluded the symphony with the third movement, the exhilarating march, everybody would go home happy.

However, so intense is the emotion of the finale, so overpowering yet so vulnerable and so deeply felt, that this final movement works structurally, although it defies all convention. A lugubrious bassoon phrase opened the first movement, and the essence of that phrase was the 'sigh' of desperation. In this last movement, bleak desolation takes over; one descending pattern remorselessly follows another. Then in the last few pages there is a final, desperate, cry for help, repeated until it dies away, a pianissimo stroke of the gong, sombre trombones, and a concluding descent into the dark orchestral colours of cellos and double-basses. One of the ever popular parlour-games of musical history is to look at the last works of certain composers, especially those who died young – Mozart, Schubert, for instance – and to speculate what sort of music they might have gone on to compose had they lived ten or twenty years longer. In the case of Tchaikovsky, such speculation is unthinkable; having written a piece such as this, all emotion is exhausted.

Nine days after the first performance, Tchaikovsky was dead. What happened? For years it was generally believed that he had died of cholera, from intentionally drinking unboiled water during an epidemic. Such rumours helped this symphony achieve instant fame when it was performed at his memorial concert a few days after he died. Tchaikovsky, people said, had prophesied his own death. Had he not composed his own requiem? Indeed, at one point in the symphony had he not quoted an actual phrase from the Requiem Mass of the Russian Orthodox Church? But the circumstances of his death are more complex. What happened came to light as recently as 1978 when the Russian scholar Alexandra Orlova revealed information unearthed in a museum in Leningrad – information that for obvious reasons had long been suppressed.

It transpires that an influential aristocrat had written a letter accusing Tchaikovsky of a homosexual relationship with the man's nephew. The letter was addressed to the Tsar himself. It was to be delivered by hand by a high-ranking civil servant called Jacobi. Like Tchaikovsky, Jacobi was a former pupil of the school of jurisprudence and he feared that the damning evidence of the composer's homosexuality would not only ruin Tchaikovsky but would bring shame on the law-school. He set up a 'court of honour', which included six of Tchaikovsky's contemporaries from the school, to decide how the scandal might be averted. Tchaikovsky was summoned to appear before the 'court' on 31 October 1893. After more than five hours of deliberation they decreed that he should kill himself to save the honour of the law school and avoid the shame of personal humiliation. Two days later Tchaikovsky was mortally ill – almost certainly from arsenic poisoning. Thus, the story that he died of cholera after drinking polluted water is either a fabrication or an irrelevance.

We shall probably never know the real truth that lies behind the Pathétique, just as we shall never disentangle the fact from the fiction in Berlioz's Fantastic Symphony. But what is extraordinary is that both works, and of course many others too, can still make their impact in purely musical terms, without our needing to know the day-to-day circumstances that prompted their composition. Clearly, Tchaikovsky still talks to the great majority of the musical public in a language they can understand, directly and openly. More crucial, the 'sound' of Tchaikovsky – for good or ill – is what most people associate with 'classical music'. When today's avant-garde composers are accused of writing 'difficult' music, they are really being criticised for writing music that no longer sounds like Tchaikovsky; a gap of one hundred years has developed between the taste of the general public and most young composers writing today.

At the start of the twentieth century that schism between the creative composer and the general concert-going audience already existed. The artist has often been ahead of his audience, but in our own century the gap has widened to a chasm that seems unbridgeable. It is a curious feature of concert-life today that the only sure way to guarantee a full house is to advertise a 'Tchaikovsky night'. No composer, living or dead, can match that popular acclaim.

8
Sounds for Tomorrow?

Before the start of the 1914–18 War music was moving – had already moved – into a new era. The traditional harmonic vocabulary, on which symphonic thought and argument depended, was as dead as the dodo. Composers were to explore different paths – improvisation, *musique concrète*, shorter forms, newer and crisper sonorities.

Indeed, at the beginning of our century, Schoenberg and the 'New Viennese School' had created a musical system – finally, intentionally and, to Schoenberg, logically – on principles that seemed positively anti-symphonic; the discipline of 'serialism' where the selection of notes, the precise order in which they appear, their rhythmic interplay and, indeed, minute differences of loud and soft are all mathematically accountable and predetermined. That path – or that dead-end, depending on which camp you chose to follow – had its opponents as well as its champions. For many composers there was the opposite line of development, the totally different aesthetic that says music should be transcendental, anti-cerebral, that much would happen by chance, and the performers should be given only the gentlest clues by the composer as to the actual notes to be improvised.

Ultimately both schools of thought are in direct conflict with the entire tradition of symphonic writing, where the very *raison d'être* of the symphony is the statement, the development, the progressive exploration of music's raw materials – the presentation of a musical argument.

Arnold Schoenberg conducting. (Kapp)

These were some of the dilemmas that faced composers in America and Western Europe, where such fine arguments could be evaluated almost as philosophical abstractions. But, for a young Soviet composer, Dmitri Shostakovich, the problem was immediate and acute. He wrote fifteen symphonies, exploiting to the full the emotional power of symphonic thought and orchestral colour. And if we are considering the development of the symphony in this age of conflict and turmoil, artistic as well as political, even his detractors must admit that Shostakovich was one of the greatest masters of the form.

For Vaughan Williams, the compulsion to produce music celebrating the country he loved, in a tone specifically English, was a task

Had he written nothing else, *Fantasia on a Theme by Thomas Tallis* would have guaranteed Ralph Vaughan Williams an undisputed place in English music. But his nine symphonies assure his importance in the history of the form.

he willingly set himself without any external pressure. He was free to write in whatever idiom he felt appropriate. Similarly, Roy Harris, the American farm-boy (born coincidentally on Abraham Lincoln's birthday) could, like Aaron Copland, celebrate the aspirations of that youthful America with optimism and directness, ebullience and open ambition – everybody's dream of a new world. But the new world – certainly the new political focus of the twentieth century – lay not in America but in Russia; that, at least, was how it was perceived by many artists who saw the 1917 Revolution as a turning point.

A devotion to Russia, and to the cause of socialism, never left Shostakovich. He was born in St Petersburg in 1906 and did not start to learn the piano until he was nine, relatively old. Within a couple of years this frail, bespectacled and brilliant child could play all forty-eight preludes and fugues of Bach's Well-Tempered Clavier, for he was not only gifted but intensely hard-working, a lifelong characteristic.

Craftsmanship, always craftsmanship, was the point from which he approached his job and when he sat down to work nothing distracted him. He was determined always to be best at whatever he did, not that he was selfishly ambitious or vain, but because he simply wanted to do his best and be the best. At all times he was fully aware of the responsibility of the artist in society. On one occasion, in the dressing room after a concert, he said to his son Maxim, the conductor:

'An artist on stage is a soldier in combat. No matter how hard it is, you cannot retreat.' There are political implications in that statement which, in his case, were particularly true. The première of his First Symphony was a triumphant success. It was 1925 – only a few years after the Russian Revolution – and it marked the appearance of a nineteen-year-old composer, a confident new Russian voice with something to say and the technique with which to say it.

His name instantly became famous – in Russia, America and Europe.

Shostakovich as a young man in 1923.

Shostakovich with his
children in 1947.

Bruno Walter conducted the symphony in Berlin. Leopold Stokowski performed it in Philadelphia. Klemperer played it and so did Toscanini. From that point onwards, Shostakovich was in the limelight or – when one considers the political climate in Russia – a searchlight. The authorities watched him like a hawk. To produce such a work at the age of nineteen was staggering enough, but his musical language was astringent, satirical and dangerously dissonant, reflecting the modern trends in Western music. This was his natural voice, and in his Second Symphony, commissioned in 1927 to celebrate the tenth anniversary of the Russian Revolution, he attempted to combine a truly modern idiom with Marxist ideology.

The crunch came with his opera *Lady Macbeth of Mtsensk*. It was tremendously successful. By 1936 it had been performed eighty-three times in Leningrad and ninety-seven in Moscow, as well as in New York, Stockholm, London, Zurich and Copenhagen. At that point all hell broke loose.

On 28 January 1936 *Pravda*, the official newspaper of the Communist Party, ran a devastating editorial, declaiming: 'Chaos instead of music.' The opera was denounced as 'fidgety, screaming and neurotic; coarse, primitive and vulgar'. It was an official warning against all modernism in Soviet music. Shostakovich was attacked and ostracised by the Union of Soviet Composers. Nobody would touch his music. His fellow musicians were too terrified to defend him.

What was behind it all? There was one simple answer: Stalin had come to see the opera and had stormed out of the theatre in a rage. It now seems clear that the article in *Pravda* was dictated by Stalin himself. As a composer who had incurred official displeasure in a period when terror raged across Russia, Shostakovich was under what amounted to a death-sentence. In the Stalinist purges, people who incurred official displeasure simply disappeared overnight. Shostakovich was certain he would be arrested. He always kept a small suitcase packed and ready for the anticipated visit in the early hours of the morning. But Stalin was too clever to eliminate Shostakovich. Like all dictators, he appreciated the propaganda potential of art. Indeed, in Shostakovich, he recognised the power of music – especially in the scores composed for Soviet films and the so-called 'military' symphonies which appeared during World War II.

In 1948 Shostakovich was the subject of another attack along with Prokofiev, Khachaturian and others. In a so-called 'historical resolution' they were criticised for their 'formalistic, anti-people tendencies ... alien to the Soviet people'. The witch-hunt continued and for Shostakovich – who believed sincerely in communism and Soviet power – the irony of his position was to remain, even after the 'thaw' that followed Stalin's death in 1953.

Shostakovich belonged to the first generation of Russian composers educated entirely under the Soviet system. His loyalty to his country was unquestioned – even when his music incurred disfavour. And with fifteen symphonies to his credit he is widely regarded as the greatest symphonist of the twentieth century. These works certainly contain the most extraordinary range of emotions – from the personal anguish of the later works to the massive, epic utterances of the war. Some of these symphonies can be regarded as 'official' works, in so far as they celebrate momentous events in the history of the Soviet people, the revolutionary struggle, the memory of Lenin, and so on.

Shostakovich regarded the massive, panoramic canvas of the symphony as a richly comprehensive form – as did Mahler, who said, 'The symphony must be like the world; it must be all-embracing.' This begs the question: How do you perceive that world? To Mahler, it was often a fearsome, nightmare world of the subconscious, of hidden childhood memories, distant echoes of a village band, the sinister overtones of a bugle-call, insistent and disturbing, full of doubt and terror. To Shostakovich – working in a totalitarian regime – the problem was even more fundamental. The official line demanded optimism, con-

Silhouettes of Gustav Mahler, whose symphonies had a nightmarish quality. His understanding of the orchestra owed a great deal to the years he spent as an operatic conductor.

fidence and unremitting heroism — qualities that conflicted with his own deeply felt pessimism, his scepticism and his sense of irony and tragedy. For him there were no clear-cut solutions, no final triumphs, no slick, glib answers; only the struggle to reconcile a personal, expressive impulse with the obvious requirements of the society to which he readily acknowledged total allegiance. To Shostakovich, the composer had a moral duty to his fellow citizens. In his Fifth Symphony he set out to pull together these apparently opposed objectives.

Although he had been criticised in *Pravda*, publicly and

vehemently, for writing music that was considered 'difficult', Shostakovich suffered in silence, condemned and ostracised. When, after his Fourth Symphony was suppressed, his Fifth Symphony appeared, it became known as 'the creative reply of a Soviet artist to justified criticism' – the designation of an unknown commentator, although Shostakovich went along with it. The Fifth Symphony was a tremendous success and it reinstated him. Some Western critics immediately belittled it as a concession to political pressure, but it is no such thing. The finale of the work, admittedly, is a rousing and jubilant conclusion, optimistic and direct in its appeal. At the same time, it is clear that in this piece Shostakovich makes no concession whatever to 'Socialist Realism'. It is, as far as we can tell, a totally 'abstract' composition, built on traditional lines. It is not a propaganda piece that glorifies this or that. Neither does it celebrate tractor-drivers, factory workers, the struggle against imperialism, or anything else that would have ingratiated him in Stalin's eyes. Instead, Shostakovich modelled the piece on very clear lines, 'having come to the conclusion that a symphony is not viable unless it is architec-turally secure'. The actual musical material is certainly more accessible than some of his other works, yet at every stage this piece bears his own, unmistakable imprint, as Boris Schwarz has stated.

The work has implanted itself firmly in the imagination of the concert-going public, and has become one of the most popular sym-phonies composed in this century. The reason is simple – and it is the reason why a great number of young composers, in what can only be described as a new romanticism, return persistently to the idea of symphonic writing – because it provides a public declaration of a composer's intellectual skill and emotional power, and as such can encompass sadness, triumph, humour, meditation, grandeur – re-defining and testing its boundaries from one generation of composers to the next.

In his book *Music, Ho!* written half a century ago, the English com-poser and conductor Constant Lambert talked about 'the appalling popularity of music'. Published in 1934, in the decade that followed the creation of the BBC and the concept of public service broadcasting, the book drew attention to the omnipresent wireless and the ever-changing technology of performance. Ominously, the book carried the subtitle 'A Study of Music in Decline'. Gramophone recording had taken the art and the craft out of musical performance, turning the entire business on its head. Musical sounds which, up to then, had existed only within the time-span of a living performance, could now be 'canned' – trapped, immortalised, packaged, re-evaluated and reperformed, not by the players but by the audience. Music – the most intangible of all the arts, dying away with the final chord into the air itself – was now to be as durable as a novel or a piece of sculpture, permanently exposed to public view, ossified and unchanging. Consequently many of the conventional relationships that had existed for centuries between the composer, the performer and the audience were to disappear for ever. We – the listeners, the conductors, the composers, the interpreters, the publishers, the concert promoters, the orchestras, soloists and concert-goers – were soon to discover that the ground-rules had changed, and that our perception of music would also change, rapidly and irrevocably.

Not all of Constant Lambert's prophecies have been fulfilled; some of his predictions on symphonic and harmonic matters might now strike us as quaint. But his central theme – that music would become as ordinary and as all-surrounding as wallpaper snipped into convenient lengths and every bit as forgettable – is truer now than he could have imagined. In the process there has been an increasing

The recording and the reproduction of music has now reached the point where today's technical standards far exceed the wildest dreams of pioneers. This is an early advertisement for a portable wind-up gramophone.

tendency for music to be chopped into bite-sized, easily-digested morsels, the antithesis of symphonic style or anything requiring attention and concentration on the part of the listener.

Moreover, if music in the thirties had become 'wallpaper', today it is part of the furniture. Television, car radios, hi-fi tape players – portable, pocket-sized and personalised – are supplemented each day by a yet more bewildering array of videograms, wrist-watch TVs and other toys, as bewildering to the manufacturers gambling on which technological system to adopt as it is to the general public puzzling over which gadget to buy, confident only in the knowledge that tomorrow's development renders today's purchase as obsolete as the cat's whisker and the wind-up gramophone. Music has become portable; part and parcel of jogging, cycling and every other aspect of life; musical performance is no longer a shared experience but a private one. As we put on our headphones and switch on, we also, in another sense, switch off, retreating from the outside world and into the confines of our own skulls.

Consequently, musical performance has lost much of that sense of occasion so fundamental to our enjoyment. Most of the music Bach, Handel and later generations encountered had been composed in their own lifetime, newly commissioned, composed to order and performed, as often as not, with the ink still wet. We should also remember that before the expansion of music publishing in the nineteenth century (often in the form of piano transcriptions of operas and symphonies) it was not at all exceptional for the composer, performer and musical director to be one and the same person. Neither was it unusual, before the spread of subscription concerts, for the audience to consist exclusively of the composer's patron and his guests. A new symphony by Haydn, for example, played at Esterházy in the 1780s, would be appraised there and then on its merits. Today, if Haydn were alive, every new symphony he produced would have to compete with thousands of works by other composers, readily available from current gramophone catalogues in so-called 'authentic' performances. If we were truly honest, we would admit that there is actually little difference between one good recording and the next. Conductor X may take one section of a piece marginally quicker than Conductor Y; the recording by Maestro A may be more or less intense at certain moments than the recording by Maestro B. But by and large these differences of interpretation are trivial.

Sadly, in the effort to differentiate between yet one more top-class

Before the invention of the gramophone and the radio, all types of music were transcribed as piano duets, one of the most popular forms of domestic music-making in the nineteenth century, here depicted in a cartoon titled 'Piano-Forte'.

recording of Beethoven's Pastoral and the dozens that already exist, critics and record-reviewers resort to drawing our attention to the technical expertise of the recording itself; we no longer listen to the music but to the sound it makes. This is an extraordinary state of affairs when one considers that until recently, at least within the last two hundred years, opinions varied widely as to what was good or bad phrasing, how a trill should start and finish, or even what constituted an orchestra.

The word 'orchestra' originated in the theatrical performances of ancient Greece; it referred to the space in front of the stage, the semi-circle where the chorus danced and sang. Later on, the stage itself became known as the orchestra – the place where you would find the musicians. Similarly, in the eighteenth century, the term 'chapel' often referred not to the building, but to the musicians employed there, under the direction of the Kapellmeister, the bandmaster. Only after a long period of development did the term 'orchestra' come to signify a standard selection and grouping of instruments, as we know it today.

The idea that the nucleus of the orchestra, the primary tone-colour so to speak, should be string tone is of comparatively recent date, growing out of the courts of England and France early in the seventeenth century. In the reign of James I the royal ensemble of 'violins' (the term included violas and cellos) was used to accompany masques and festive occasions, when their numbers would be augmented. In France in 1626 Louis XIII reconstituted his players as the Vingt-quatre Violons du Roi. It was copied in London when Charles II came to the throne in 1660.

Other princely courts, in Austria and Germany, maintained ensembles on the model of Versailles. There the music was in the capable hands of the charismatic music director, Jean-Baptiste Lully. It was largely due to Lully's influence that the playing and the manufacture of woodwind instruments made such great strides – the achievement of two families of instrument-makers, Chédeville and Hotteterre. They modified the old Renaissance designs and flutes, recorders, oboes and bassoons became more reliable, more flexible in phrasing and agility, more evenly in tune, and with the tone-colour more consistent throughout an extended range of notes.

Thus, at the start of the eighteenth century the basic tone-colour of the violins, violas and cellos acquired greater variety and piquancy as pairs of oboes and bassoons became standard in the ensemble. A continuo instrument – usually a harpsichord – was another essential ingredient, its function being to keep time and fill in the harmony. Clarinets took longer to establish their role; Haydn, for example, did not include them in a symphony until 1793.

In the brass department the trombones took even longer than the clarinets to gain an accepted place in the ensemble, principally because they had for centuries been associated with church music. In opera they were associated with moments of great solemnity, often conjuring up the supernatural. But trumpets and kettledrums, often co-opted from the local militia or town guild, carried no such sacred aura and were soon to establish themselves in eighteenth-century orchestras.

The role of the keyboard continuo persisted right through the eighteenth century. In London Haydn 'presided at the pianoforte' when his symphonies were performed at the Salomon concerts in Hanover Square in the 1790s. Indeed, the presence of a keyboard instrument was taken for granted, even when no special part for it appears in the score. But towards the end of the eighteenth century the keyboard continuo declined in importance, as pairs of hunting

— 155 —

horns proved ideally suited to taking over the continuo role of filling in the harmony. Simultaneously the job of the violinist-conductor grew more important. For generations, the principal violinist had shared with the keyboard player the task of 'conducting' the upper and lower 'voices' of the orchestra – as had Salomon and Haydn. But during the nineteenth century the growing complexity of orchestral music gave rise to the 'star' conductor. In time, the violin bow was replaced by the conductor's baton, or a rolled-up scroll of music paper, or simply the hands and fingers; the conductor Leopold Stokowski abandoned the use of the baton after 1929.

At the end of the eighteenth century 'the orchestra' consisted of two flutes, two oboes, two clarinets, two bassoons, two or four horns, two trumpets, timpani and strings; the chart on page 12 compares different orchestras at different periods. It will be noticed that in the nineteenth century orchestras grew to enormous proportions with the addition of instruments extending the compass of playable notes: piccolo, cor anglais, E-flat and bass clarinets, double-bassoon and so on. At the same time the standard instruments improved in many respects. Ways were found of increasing the string tension which added brilliance and volume to violins, violas, cellos and double-basses, while the new Tourte bow, developed towards the end of the eighteenth century by the French family of bowmakers, gave greater agility and subtlety of sound. In the woodwind department the Boehm system of design completely revolutionised flutes, oboes and clarinets in the first half of the nineteenth century. Horns and trumpets also improved with mechanisms that enabled them to be played with ease in different keys, through the addition of valves that raised and lowered the basic 'bugle notes'.

For years, these newer models co-existed with the old-fashioned varieties but, in time, players and composers adopted the attitude that everything was possible, however fast, however loud, however complicated. If no suitable instrument existed, then, with the arrogance and enterprise of the nineteenth century, it was time to invent it. Wagner increased the size of the woodwind section and demanded new instruments – a set of tubas, for instance – to be made, not merely to increase the volume of sound but also to give a wider and more subtle range of tone-colours. Richard Strauss, supreme master of the orchestral palette, took these forces to their limit. Like so many conductor-composers, Strauss acquired his brilliance and confidence as an orchestrator from the day-to-day experience of standing in front

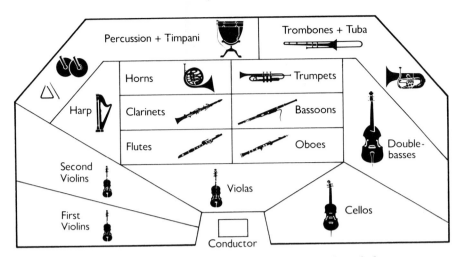

A standard disposition of a modern symphony orchestra.

of the players and discovering what worked and what did not.

With the twentieth century came a massive increase in the size of 'the kitchen' – the traditional term for the percussion department. The piano, used as a percussive instrument, has reclaimed a position in the modern orchestra and the celesta, a keyboard instrument with a delicate bell-like sound, was established once and for all the moment that Tchaikovsky used it in 1892 in the Dance of the Sugar-Plum Fairy in his ballet *The Nutcracker*. But in the twentieth century every conceivable object has been added to the department that originally provided only the 'Turkish' exotica of triangle, cymbal and bass-drum: sandpaper blocks, typewriters, wind machines, anvils, chains, whistles and anything else that can bang, twang or thud, shake, rattle or roll. To walk around the warehouse of a firm that specialises in the hire of percussion instruments is to visit an Aladdin's cave, where gongs, shakers and scrapers from the Far East, Africa and the West Indies provide endless hours of innocent amusement.

But in our own age electronics, tape-recording and synthesisers have brought the most important developments in orchestration. Even before the 1920s, composers explored gramophone recordings – played forwards, backwards, fast and slow – in a cumbersome and frustrating attempt to organise prerecorded sounds. But after World War II the appearance of the domestic tape-recorder made *musique concrète* a development to be reckoned with. Recordings were made of dustbin lids, political speeches, heartbeats and breaking glass. Distorted, chopped up, and combined with each other, they were listened to by composers with long, serious faces. These antics have now been taken over by students in art colleges, since composers, meanwhile, have roamed deeper and deeper into the territory of synthesisers, computers, multichannel recording and overdubbing one sound on top of another. In the world of rock music, where much of the most imaginative work is done, these techniques have revolutionised the entire nature of orchestration and composition, the very antithesis of traditional methods. No longer is it necessary for a composer to invent sounds in his head and then write them down; instead, music is built up by trial and error, layer upon layer in the recording studio, and the end-product is not a musical score that others may perform, but an audio or video tape where the recording itself *is* the musical composition.

Karlheinz Stockhausen. After World War II tape-recording presented new possibilities to composers such as Stockhausen, who often combined 'live' orchestral performance with prerecorded sounds.

Just as the concert grand piano has been regarded as an 'improvement' on the harpsichord and the electronic organ as a logical development of a bellows-operated church organ, it is equally tempting to regard this electronic revolution as merely another development, logical and timely, in the field of orchestration; extra colours on the composer's palette, so to speak. But its significance is much greater than that. Far from enriching the expressive capabilities of music (as the

addition of valves can be said to have broadened the capabilities of the basic hunting-horn) recording has in fact limited our choice in many ways.

Any professional orchestra today, paradoxically, regularly needs to make successful recordings to attract audiences to 'live' concerts, by maintaining the orchestra's prestige amongst others of world class competing in the same league. These recordings usually duplicate the same few dozen standard symphonies and concertos that recur

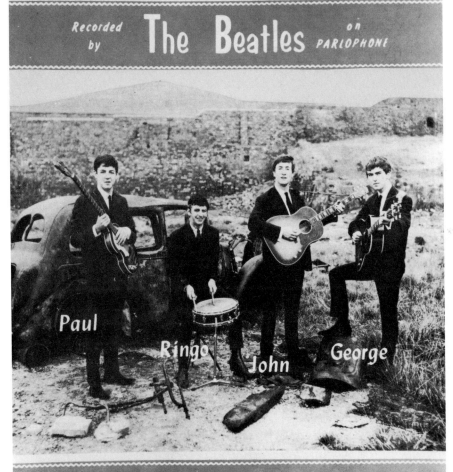

Although they disbanded in 1970, the Beatles had brought new lyricism, compassion, vitality and experimentation to pop music.

monotonously in concert programmes – the masterpieces of Beethoven, Brahms, Dvořák, and other composers who died many years ago.

This is an odd state of affairs. In past centuries, most concerts consisted of music by contemporary figures. Today, and for some time, the circumstances have been reversed; our dilemma is that so little of the music we hear (apart from pop music, which is designed to be disposable) comes from our own century. On the contrary, we are permitted a privilege denied all previous generations; with the flick of a switch we have access to 'great' music from all periods of musical history, stretching back to the Middle Ages and beyond. These works survive in many cases not because their inherent qualities render them imperishable but simply because we possess the technology to preserve them indefinitely and cannot bear to throw anything away.

In the process of saving the old, we have built up a Euro-mountain of music, an impenetrable barrier to anything new: any new piece of music needs to fight to get a hearing at all. If a young composer thinks instinctively in terms of the sonorities of a conventional symphony orchestra, then he must face up to the fact that he is not merely competing with his contemporaries and his immediate predecessors, but with every major composer who ever set ink on paper. Brahms once said that the reason it took him so long to produce his first symphony was that he felt intimidated by the achievement of Beethoven. Were he alive today, Brahms would have rather more than one intimidating predecessor to contend with.

This is one reason why the very language of music, the basic vocabulary, has changed so rapidly and fundamentally this century. Creative artists have always been ahead of their audiences. In this century the rate of musical innovation has accelerated wildly as it has in all the arts, and the gap between the composer and his audience has widened to a chasm. Fighting shy of the stultifying comparison with earlier 'classical' figures the young composer often feels tempted to ape outrageous novelties and to ignore the public completely. Very often such music is composed not to delight an audience, but to impress fellow composers. Concerts of new music, restricted entirely to such compositions, only reinforce what the English composer Richard Rodney Bennett has termed the 'ghetto mentality' – tortured intellectuals playing up to a small clique of fellow sufferers.

Inevitably, because our ears are so attuned to the music of the eighteenth and nineteenth centuries, we find it increasingly difficult

The subtle interplay of colours to be found in Debussy's orchestral work recalls the techniques of Impressionist painters, several of whom were his friends.

to accept the music of our own time. This attitude is reinforced by the policy of the larger record companies and the managements of our symphony orchestras. They say that the quickest way to go out of business is to put on programmes of contemporary music. Until the finances of major orchestras improve there is little incentive to risk programming untried works that require a great deal of costly rehearsal and alienate the public. It is a sad fact that less than twenty years away from the next century we still have not come to terms

'Just as modern poetry surely took root in certain of Baudelaire's poems, so one is justified in saying that modern music is awakened by L'après-midi d'un faune' – Pierre Boulez. This manuscript is dated 1899 and is inscribed to Debussy's mistress. Subsequently it was acquired by the pianist Alfred Cortot.

with our own. Indeed, we have assumed the role of museum curators, charged with the task of keeping popular 'masterworks' on permanent display, lacking the courage, the budgets and the space to take on anything new.

It can of course be argued that the archive value of music recordings justifies everything; that we have not only a desire but a duty to preserve the interpretations of 'masterworks' performed by our foremost conductors, orchestras and soloists. Indeed, the clarity, richness and impact of sound recording seems to have reached a standard that cannot be surpassed. It is touching to remember how, only fifty years ago, musicians such as Sir Edward Elgar laboured with enormous enthusiasm to achieve recordings in appalling and anti-musical studio conditions, so entrancing was the novelty of preserving sounds at all. The musicianship of those artists, the skill of the engineers working with the most primitive equipment, and the overpowering musicianship of the playing, evoke nothing but admiration and wonder. For example, the 1932 recording of the Elgar Violin Concerto still justifies its place in the current catalogue in competition with dozens of rival modern recordings, for we cherish the combination of the veteran composer and the child prodigy, Yehudi Menuhin. Similarly, with the Beatrice Harrison version of the same composer's Cello Concerto – also still available – we can listen to the performance, warts and all, because the insight these artists bring to the music outweighs any shortcomings in the technical quality of the recordings.

The archive importance of such recordings is particularly important when the performance has been conducted by the composer. The argument begins to wear thin, however, when one considers that any good recording by any distinguished soloist or orchestra playing under an acclaimed conductor must eventually and inevitably acquire *some* archive value. Consequently, the record industry has faced for some time the insoluble problem of what to preserve and what to delete; with hundreds of new recordings appearing every month, the market reached saturation long ago, and it is not at all unusual that a famous conductor will be embarking on a boxed set of Beethoven for a second or third time. This policy is financially attractive to record companies, but it has produced another substantial change in the way we perceive music: we no longer listen to Beethoven's 'Eroica' but to Giulini's 'Eroica', or Karajan's or Bernstein's.

There is also a profound difference of experience between 'canned' and 'live' music, the distinction between sitting at home listening to

Sir Edward Elgar conducting the young Yehudi Menuhin.

Sir Edward Elgar at a recording session with cellist Beatrice Harrison in 1920, in the days when the musical sounds needed to be 'aimed' at cumbersome horn microphones.

a recording and going in person to hear the same artists at a public concert. The act of attending a performance involves the audience in that performance. Most symphonies, and certainly most concertos, conclude in a manner so positive that it is clear the composer set out to provoke riotous applause – an entirely human response – the justifiable accolade for all that hard work and genius. This is a dimension that most studio recordings deny us. Many compositions demand applause and when Verdi or Puccini write a top C for the hero, it is for the very good reason that it will thrill a packed auditorium and provoke an instinctive response. Without an audience, the music loses half its impact; a 'show-stopper' only works if it stops the show.

The tragedy of so much twentieth-century music is that it has shunned that bond of contact between performer and audience, implied in the term 'performance'. When the American composer John Cage produced a piece entitled *4 Minutes, 33 Seconds* (where a performer comes on to the platform and, for precisely that duration, plays absolutely nothing at all, then exits) he questioned many of our most cherished preconceptions and prejudices. His point was that music has as much to do with the listeners as with the performers, that the ambience and attitudes of the audience are part and parcel of the music, and – in the last analysis – 'everything we do is music'. Inevitably, such an extreme attitude has invited accusations of charlatanism, but it is undeniable that music affects us and that the applause which

John Cage has been profoundly influenced by the study of Buddhism and other Eastern philosophies and some of his compositions introduce elements of chance. The son of an inventor, he has been at the forefront of many avant-garde developments.

To extend the range of percussive effects, Cage inserted various objects between the strings of his 'prepared' pianos.

rounds off a concert is the natural outcome of events. We, the audience, looked forward to the occasion. We made the effort to buy tickets, to travel to the concert-hall, park the car, buy a programme, find our seat, fold up our coat and applaud the conductor as he walked on to the platform. We set out to enjoy the symphony concert, and enjoy it we shall. Had we stayed at home and come across that per-formance – perhaps by accident – on television or radio, our response would have been different. For one thing it would be less committed, less enthusiastic, less tolerant; if we didn't like it, we would simply have switched it off.

In the captivity of the concert-hall, we are denied that freedom of choice. Indeed, it takes extraordinary courage to storm out of the Royal Festival Hall in mid-symphony if the music is not to our liking. Not wishing to cause a scene, we will sit through the work to the bitter end – at home we would have switched it off long ago – and though we doze from boredom in the slow movement, we may wake up thrilled when the finale starts. Like it or loathe it, our span of attention has been stretched.

More to the point, it is only by sitting through to the end of a new piece that we can start to comprehend the composer's total design, the symphonic qualities of the score and its architectural scale. It is only by listening to the entire piece, first note to last, that we come to recognise – consciously or subconsciously – how certain patterns of rhythm or melody connect one with another. Without giving it a complete hearing its symphonic nature will elude us. Alternatively, having sat through a complete performance we may reach the opposite conclusion – that it's all a crashing bore. Either way, the music has been given a chance to prove itself on its own terms without adjusting the volume, the treble and bass, or being interrupted by a telephone call, or switching it off completely the moment our concentration flags.

There has been a growing tendency since the advent of film and television for our powers of concentration to diminish. This fact has serious implications for music composed on symphonic proportions; there is the simple danger that we will fidget and become inattentive, feeling that it is all going on a bit too long. Living in a world of communications bedevilled by pictures and dominated by journalists, we have become attuned to the snappy statement, the clipped and facile summing-up and the terse, insistent inner rhythm of newsreel film and the tabloid newspaper. These directly oppose the spacious sense of architecture that we associate with symphonic writing. One of the earliest and most fascinating experiments in this area was the film *Fantasia* (1940), which combined the talents of Walt Disney and Leopold Stokowski. Both men wanted to extend the frontiers of their particular world: Disney's skill as a cartoonist and film animator is legendary; Stokowski explored acoustics, recording techniques and

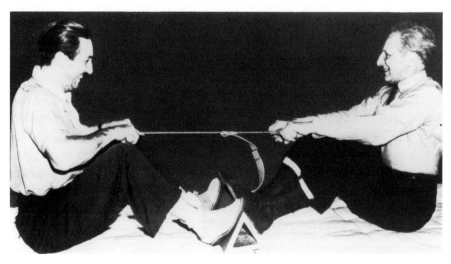

In their respective fields – musical acoustics and cartoon animation – Leopold Stokowski (right) and Walt Disney were both pioneers. *Fantasia* was the outcome of their collaboration.

different seating arrangements on concert platforms to achieve different sonorities. However, their partnership on *Fantasia* was only partially successful, not least because the combination of symphonic music and cartoon-animation involves a perilous marriage of opposites; the two disciplines achieve their effect by utterly different means.

It was a period when many musicians regarded the sound-film as an exciting new art-form, where the combination of music and images presented novel opportunities for collaboration. There were, indeed, many notable achievements, such as the film *Alexander Nevsky*. Two giants – Eisenstein, the director, and Prokofiev, the composer – collaborated to unify music and images. In America, each major film studio retained on its payroll at least one permanent symphony orchestra, consisting of the many conservatoire-trained musicians who had fled Europe in the 1930s. For a time in Britain, composers such as Arthur Bliss, William Walton and Ralph Vaughan Williams worked alongside such film-makers as Alexander Korda and Laurence Olivier. All too often, however, the narrative priorities of the film script reduced the stature of the music: while a film-maker's sequences are essentially episodic, composers think in larger paragraphs; thus, working on a symphonic and purely musical level, it is intensely frustrating when bars have to be cut or added to fit the action of the film. Music has its own rules and its own powers of language which reach beyond rational thought and the limitations of one image or the next. Unlike the visual arts, it need feel no obligation to imitate the 'real' world. Unlike the literary and dramatic arts it does not have to tell a story, and in each generation it has a way of adopting the sounds and forms best suited to its time, however contradictory these may seem.

Ralph Vaughan Williams, for example, was an English symphonist who resolutely maintained his national tone of voice. He studied, collected and totally absorbed in his own vocabulary the folk-songs of his native country, impervious to the latest fads of the avant-garde. It is that quality that makes his music endearing, touchingly personal and tremendously powerful. Of his nine symphonies, the more violent ones – the Fourth and the Sixth – are those which, so to speak, 'travel well' and are best known abroad, with their anxiety and intensity. But it is equally true that the power of his musical thought lies just as strongly in his inward, meditative and contemplative moments, where his quality of 'Englishness' is apparent from the very first notes.

His music has about it a generous, expansive, open-air feeling. Like his American counterpart Roy Harris – whose Third Symphony is one of the few truly American symphonies – he admired the poetry of Walt Whitman, and thought naturally in terms of his national identity, expressed on a broad symphonic canvas.

Theirs was the last generation of symphonists to retain any real sense of national identity. Many American composers came to study in Europe, particularly with Nadia Boulanger, whom few composers seem to have escaped. The music of younger twentieth-century composers has tended to develop a lingua franca, a sort of musical Esperanto, where the sounds and clichés may be grouped under technical headings rather than any nationalistic 'school'. As nationalism declined, other 'isms' flourished. Thus, from Paris to Cologne, from Darmstadt to IRCAM and from tape-loops to computers, traditional ideas of a symphonic language have been driven out by atonalism, serialism, minimalism and so on, each of which, in its way, resents,

Composer, teacher and conductor Nadia Boulanger was the first woman to conduct a symphony orchestra in London. She attracted to her composition classes in Paris several generations of musicians from all parts of the world – especially America. Her extraordinary dynamism made her one of the formative influences of twentieth-century music.

Pierre Boulez, the French composer, conductor and theorist, has developed the principle of 'total serialisation', in which many elements of the composition – the pitch and duration of notes, even the tone colour – are governed by a fixed permutation.

avoids and contradicts the burden of the past. The symphonic heritage, it is argued, has had its day. For many years a number of sane and sensible musicians have declared that large-scale symphonic composition, with its rich use of the orchestra, has nothing more to offer; the symphony is no longer a valid musical form; Brahms, Mahler, Bruckner, Elgar, Sibelius and the rest have said all that remains to be said.

Time will tell.

Further Reading

ABRAHAM, G. *The tradition of western music* (Oxford University Press, 1974, o.p.).

ANDERSON, E. *The letters of Mozart and his family*, n.e. prepared by A. Hyatt King (Macmillan, 1966, o.p.).

CAIRNS, P. *Memoirs of Hector Berlioz* (Panther, n.e. pbk, 1970; Gollancz, n.e. 1977).

CARSE, A. *The orchestra in the XVIII century* (Heffer, 1950, o.p.).

GEIRINGER, K. *Instruments in the history of western music* (Allen & Unwin, 1978).

HOGWOOD, C. *Music at court* (Gollancz, 1980).

HOGWOOD, C. *Haydn's visits to London* (Folio Society, 1980, o.p.).

HUTCHINGS, A. *Mozart, the man and the musician* (Thames and Hudson, 1976).

LANDON, H. C. ROBBINS. *Beethoven, a documentary study* (World of Art, Thames and Hudson, abr. ed., 1974).

LANDON, H. C. ROBBINS. *Haydn, a documentary study* (Thames and Hudson, 1981).

MANN, W. *James Galway's music in time* (Mitchell Beazley, 1982).

RABY, P. *Fair Ophelia: Harriet Smithson Berlioz* (Cambridge University Press, 1982).

RAYNOR, H. *A social history of music: from the middle ages to Beethoven* (Barrie and Jenkins, 1972, o.p.).

WESTRUP, J. A. *An introduction to musical history* (Hutchinson University Library, Hutchinson, 2nd ed., 1973, o.p.).

Picture Acknowledgements

Colour

ARCHIV FUR KUNST UND GESCHICHTE. BERLIN pages 83 top, 94 top & 98; BAYERISCHE VERWALTUNG DER STAATL. SCHLOSSER, GARTEN UND SEEN. SCHLOSS NYMPHENBURG. MUNICH page 86; BEETHOVENHAUS. BONN page 97; BRITISH MUSEUM pages 88 & 95; C. M. DIXON page 94 bottom; PHOTOGRAPHIE GIRAUDON (Prague. National Gallery) page 87 & (Musée Carnavalet) page 99; JOHN HILLELSON AGENCY (photo Erich Lessing/ Magnum) page 95 top; HISTORISCHES MUSEUM DER STADT. WIEN page 100; KUNST-HISTORISCHES MUSEUM. WIEN page 85; MOZART MUSEUM. SALZBURG page 84 top left & bottom, page 93; MUSEES NATIONAUX (Palace of Versailles) pages 81 & 82 & (Louvre) front cover; ROYAL COLLEGE OF MUSIC. LONDON both page 96; SCALA. FIRENZE (Alte Pinakothek. Munich) page 83 bottom, (Mozart Museum. Salzburg) page 84 top right, (Academia. Venice) page 89, (Louvre. Paris) pages 90, 91 & 97 bottom, (Villa Medici. Rome) page 99; STAATL. LIEGENSCHAFTSAMT. HEIDELBERG page 92.

Black and white

ARCHIV DER GESELLSCHAFT DER MUSIKFREUNDE IN WIEN page 150; ARCHIV FUR KUNST UND GESCHICHTE. BERLIN pages 27 top & 118; ERICH AUERBACH page 169; BEETHOVEN-HAUS. BONN pages 74 left & 107; BIBLIOTECA APOSTOLICA VATICANA page 19 top right; BIBLIOTHEQUE NATIONALE. PARIS page 14; BILDARCHIV DER OSTERREICHISCHEN NATIONALBIBLIOTHEK. WIEN pages 21, 79 & 132; BILDARCHIV PREUSSISCHER KULTUR-BESITZ. BERLIN page 19 bottom; BRAUNSCHWEIGISCHES LANDESMUSEUM page 103; BBC HULTON PICTURE LIBRARY pages 27 bottom, 61, 74 right, 105, 120 top & 160 (photos Bettmann Archive), 146 & 163 bottom; BRITISH LIBRARY pages 76 & 80; BRITISH MUSEUM page 58; PHOTOGRAPHIE BULLOZ pages 115 & (Carpentras Museum) 125 top; DEUTSCHE STAATSBIBLIOTHEK. BERLIN. DDR pages 49 & (Music Department) 101; DEUTSCHE FOTOTHEK. DRESDEN (Robert Schumann Museum. Zwickau) page 126 bottom; MARY EVANS PICTURE LIBRARY pages 24, 36 & 125 bottom; FOTOMAS INDEX page 31; JOHN FREEMAN & CO page 110; RONALD GRANT COLLECTION page 152; HACHETTE. (Bibliothèque de l'Opéra. Paris) page 122; PETER HARRAP/REPORT page 158; HAYDN MUSEUM. EISENSTADT page 53; HISTORISCHES MUSEUM DER STADT. WIEN page 54; HENRY E. HUNTINGTON LIBRARY & ART GALLERY page 34; DICK JAMES MUSIC LTD page 159; HERBERT VON KARAJAN COLLECTION. SALZBURG (photo Farb-Foto-Frank) page 69; RICHARD MACNUTT LTD page 112 right; RAYMOND MANDER & JOE MITCHENSON THEATRE COLLECTION page 113; MANSELL COLLECTION pages 17, 78, 120 bottom & 126 top; ROBERTO MASOTTI page 164; ANTHONY MARSHALL back cover; YEHUDI MENU-HIN page 163 top; NATIONAL ARCHIVES OF HUNGARY page 65; NOVOSTI PRESS AGENCY pages 135, 147 & 148; PERFORMING ART SERVICES. N.Y. page 165; PIERPONT MORGAN LIBRARY. N.Y. page 161; REBOUL – H. BERLIOZ COLLECTION page 108; H. ROGER-VIOLLET pages 154 & 168; ROYAL ACADEMY OF MUSIC. LONDON page 140; ROYAL COLLEGE OF

MUSIC. LONDON pages 16, 63, 112 left & 145; SALZBURGERMUSEUM CAROLINO AUGUSTEUM pages 29 & 38; SCALA. FIRENZE (Bologna Museo Civico. Bibl. Musicale) page 30; S.P.A.D.E.M. page 140; VICTORIA & ALBERT MUSEUM. LONDON page 52; WAGNER MUSEUM. BAYREUTH page 117; WEIDENFELD & NICOLSON ARCHIVE pages 116 & (Wagner Museum. Bayreuth) 119; Photographs on pages 137 & 138 are from *Tschaikowski* by Staatl. Haus-Museum. Klin.

The table on page 12 and the diagrams on pages 60 & 157 are reproduced from *The New Grove Dictionary of Music and Musicians* (1980/81) by permission of Macmillan Press Ltd, London.